Sapporo City, Japan

A TRAVEL PHOTO ART BOOK

LAINE CUNNINGHAM

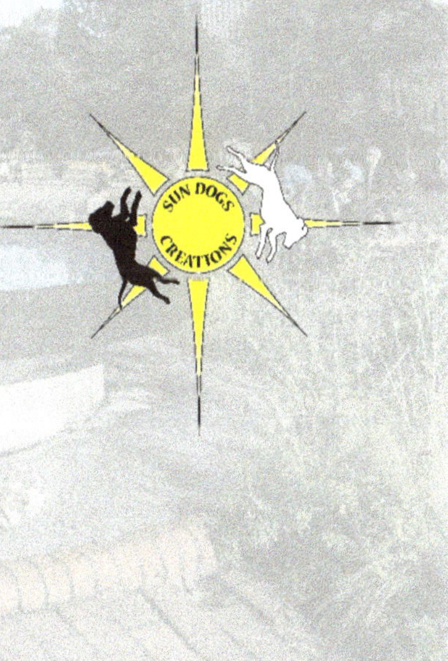

Sapporo City, Japan

A Travel Photo Art Book

Published by Sun Dogs Creations
Changing the World One Book at a Time
Print ISBN: 978-1-951389-29-1

Cover Image by Laine Cunningham
Cover Design by Angel Leya

Known as much for its summertime activities as its annual snow festival, Sapporo is the fifth largest city in Japan. The downtown district is divided by the mile-long Odori Park, a strip dotted with flower gardens, fountains, and plenty of benches. Other areas of the city are beautified by Shinto shrines and the Toyohira River.

The city is the capital of the Hokkaido district, an area known for being Japan's premier food location. With coastal access to the Sea of Japan, the Sea of Okhotsk, and the Pacific Ocean, the district provides seafood lovers with the greatest variety and the freshest options in the entire country. Its historical flocks of sheep made Jingisukan, or lamb BBQ, one of its signature dishes. The locally produced dairy is famous for its rich mouthfeel, so indulge in ice cream after sampling a signature bowl of miso-based ramen.

From Susukino's entertainment district to the TV tower, Sapporo has a lot to offer at any time of the year.

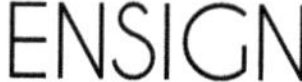
ENSIGN

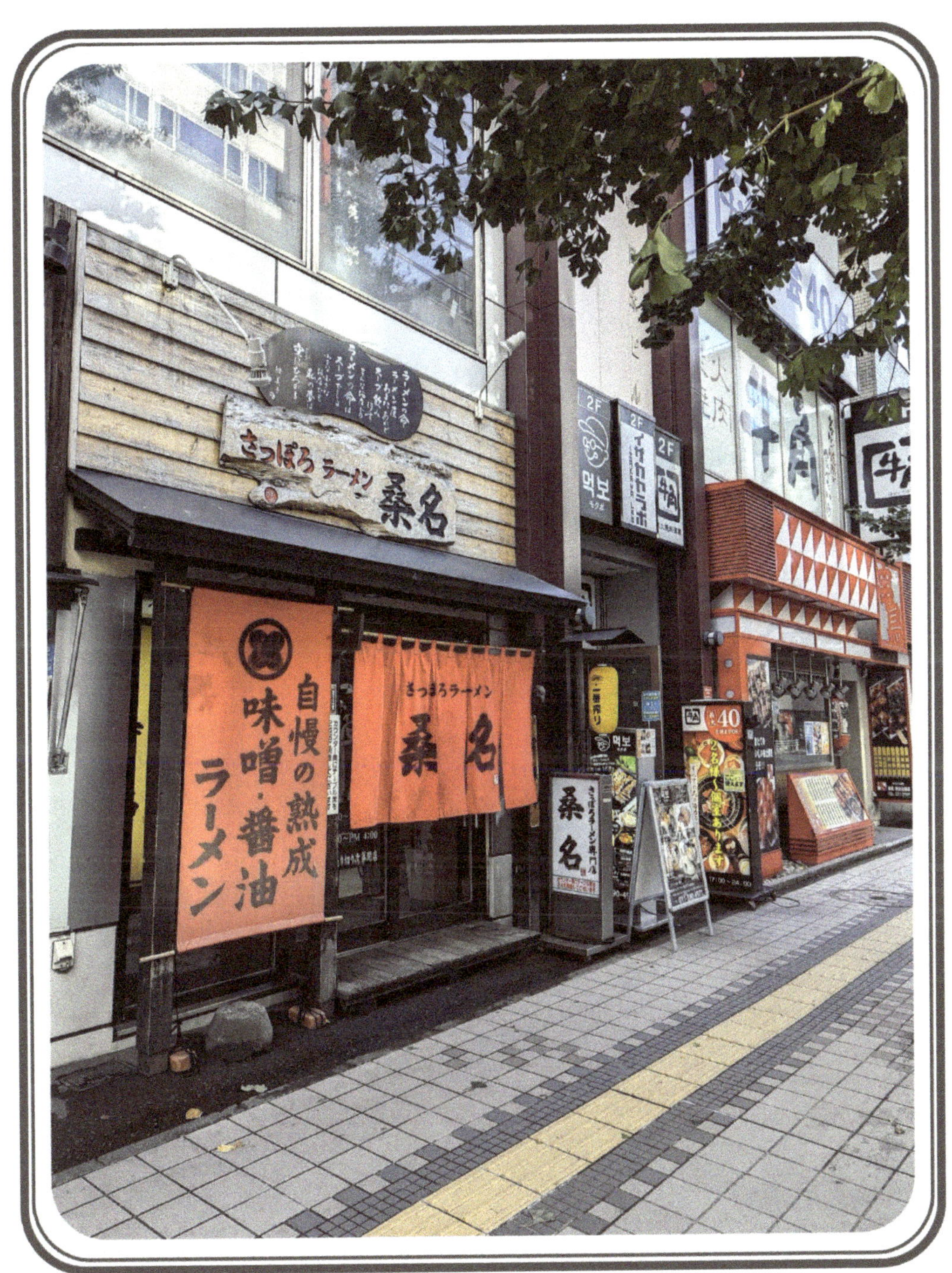

さっぽろ ラーメン 桑名
自慢の熟成
味噌・醤油
ラーメン
さっぽろラーメン
桑名
桑名
さっぽろラーメン専門店
2F
먹보
2F
2F

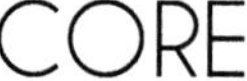
CORE

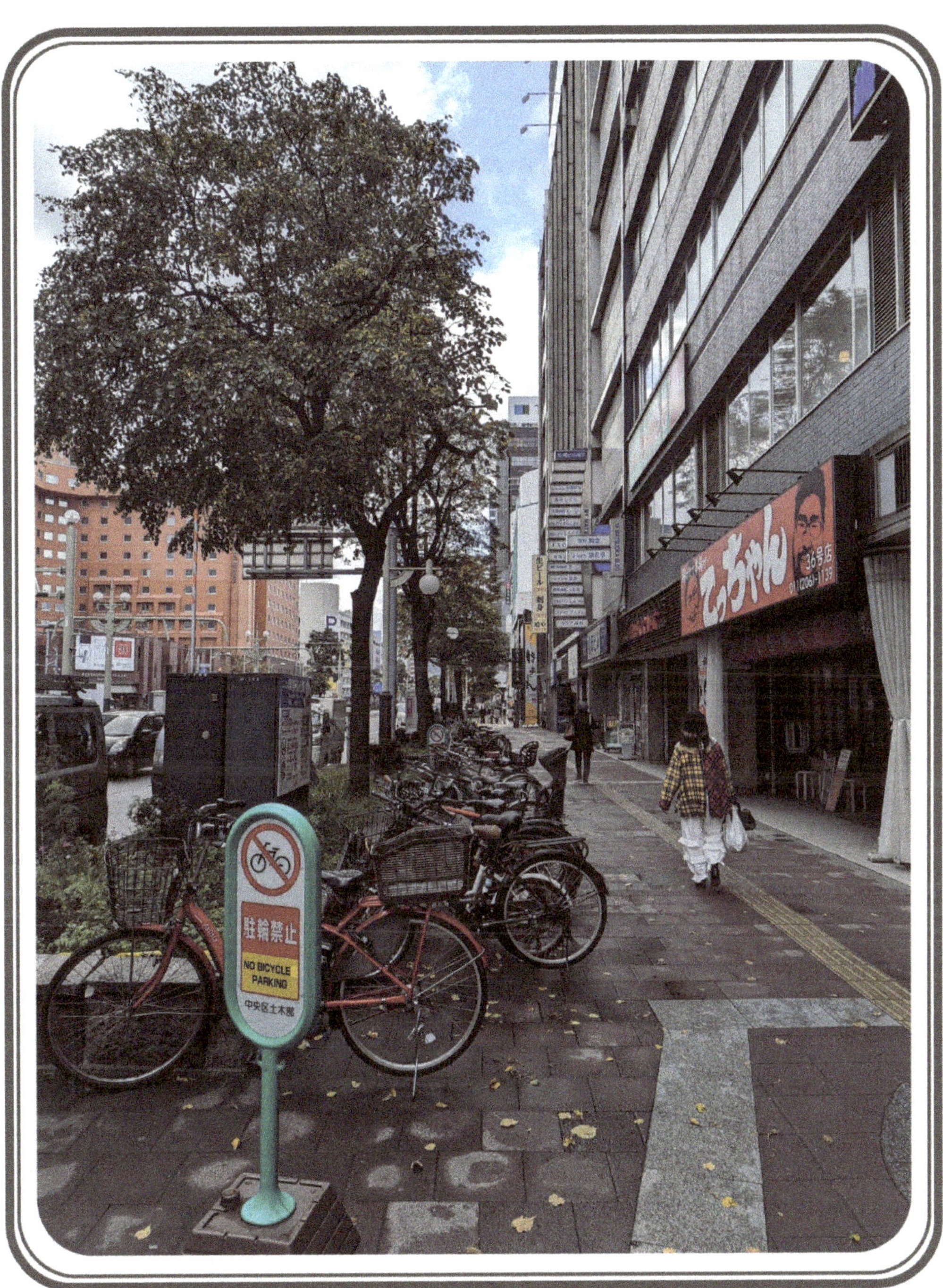
駐輪禁止
NO BICYCLE PARKING
中央区土木部
てっちゃん
36号店

IRON BOY

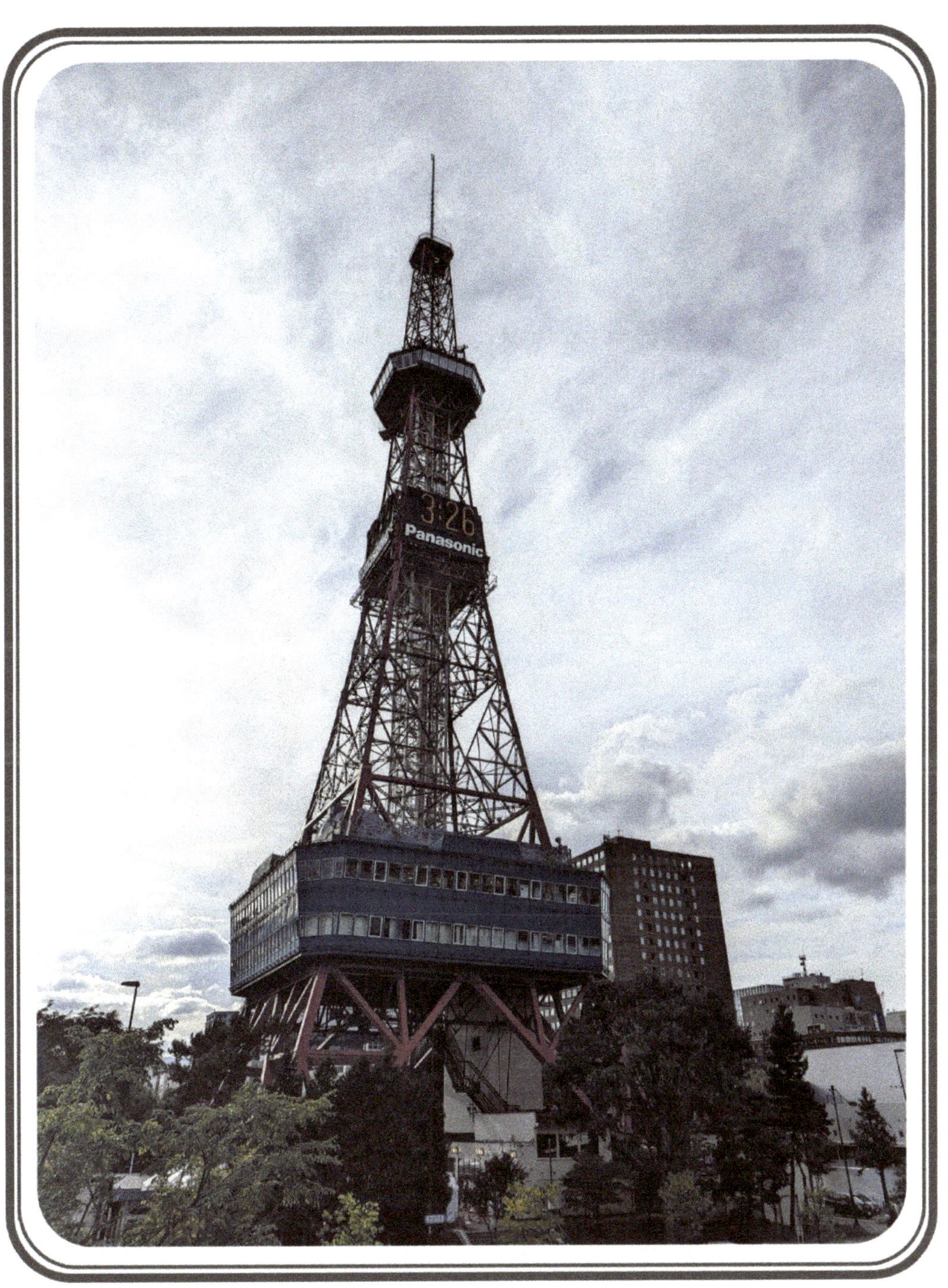
3:26
Panasonic

ESCAPE

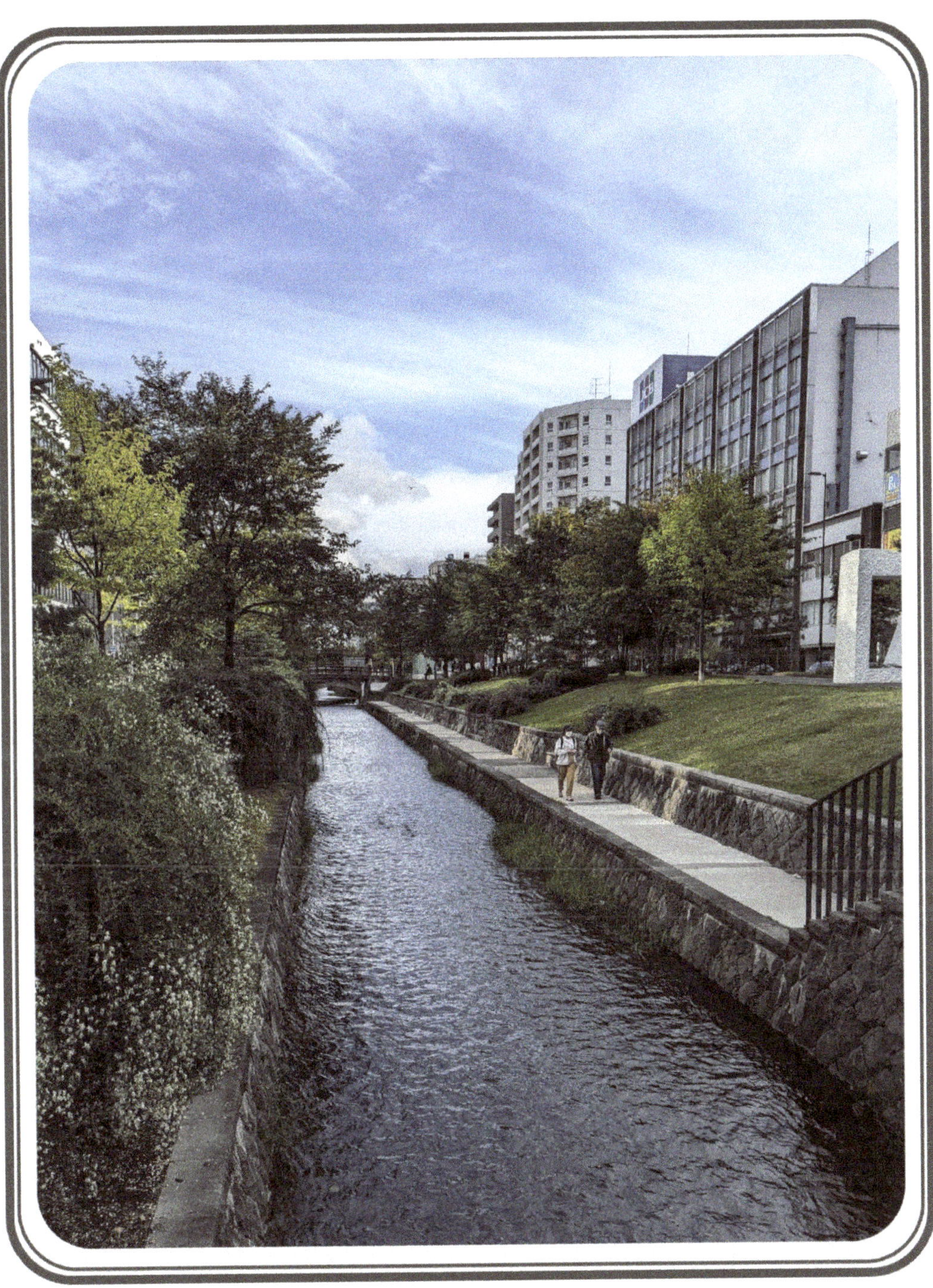

MOTHERSHIP

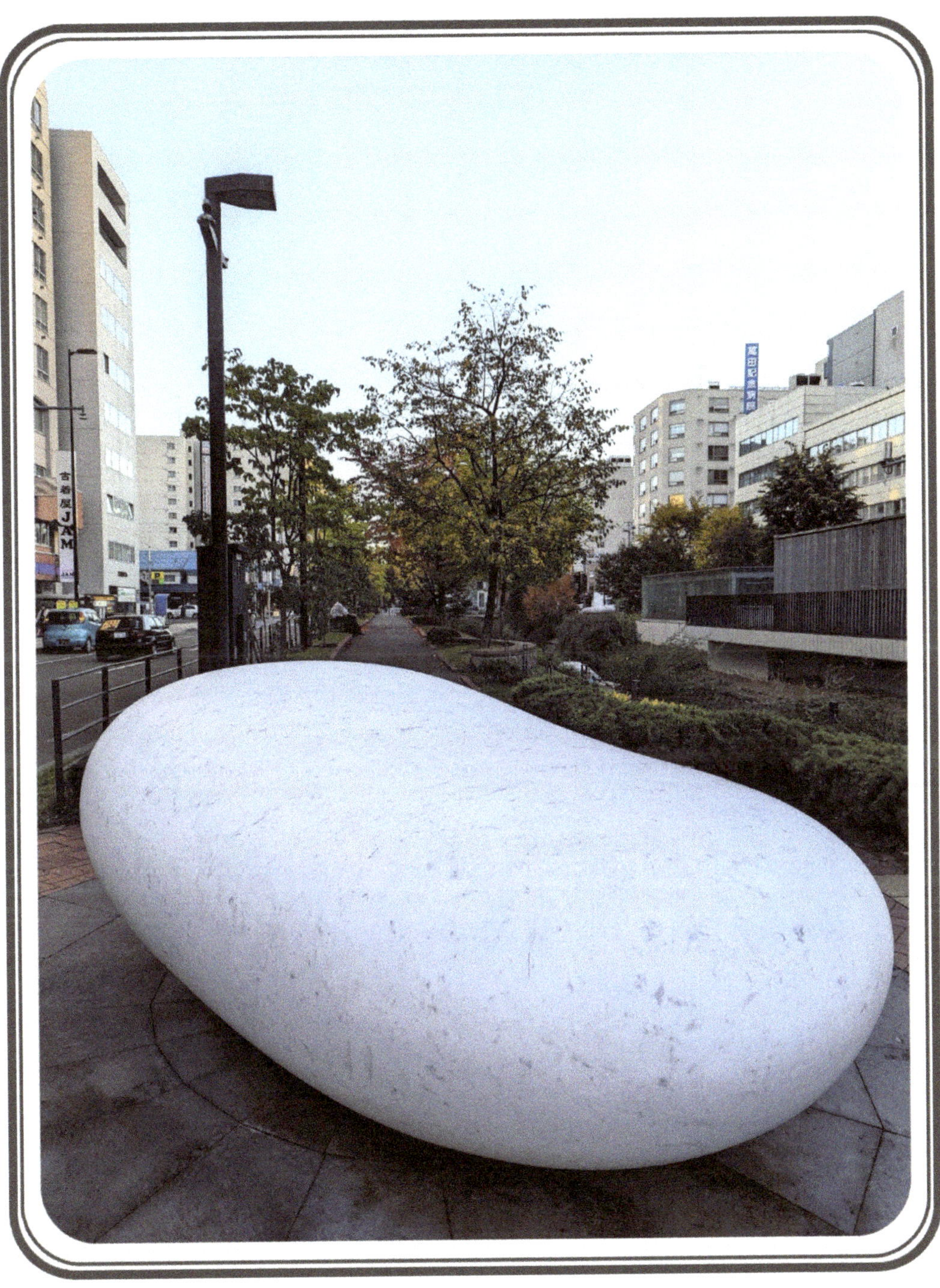
古着屋JAM

LATH

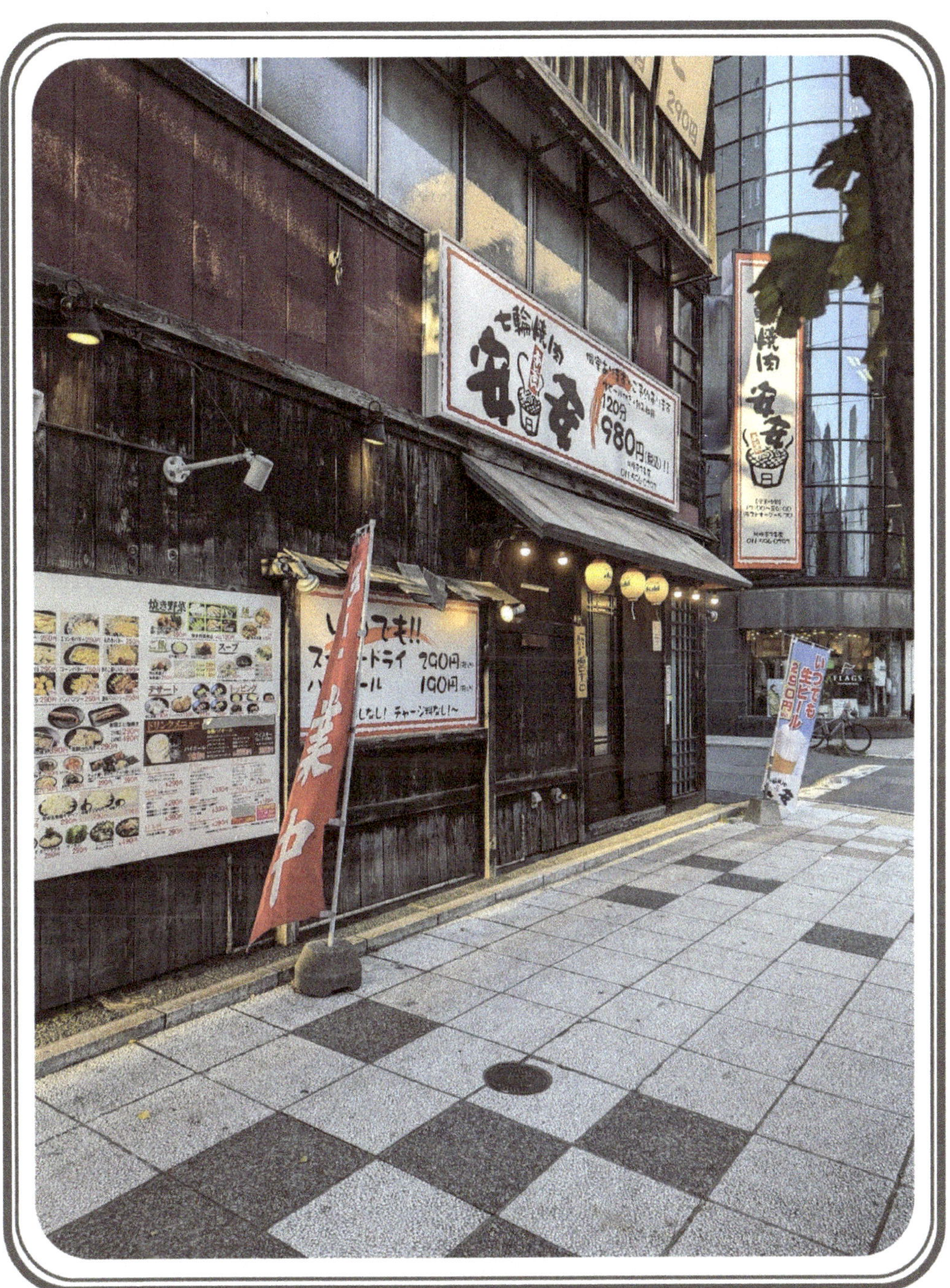
七輪焼肉
安安
120分
980円(税込)!!
焼肉
安安
いつでも!!
290円
190円
チャージ料なし!~
いつでも
生ビール
290円

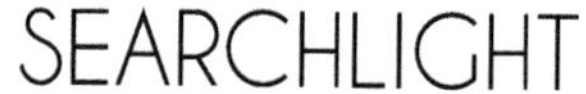
SEARCHLIGHT

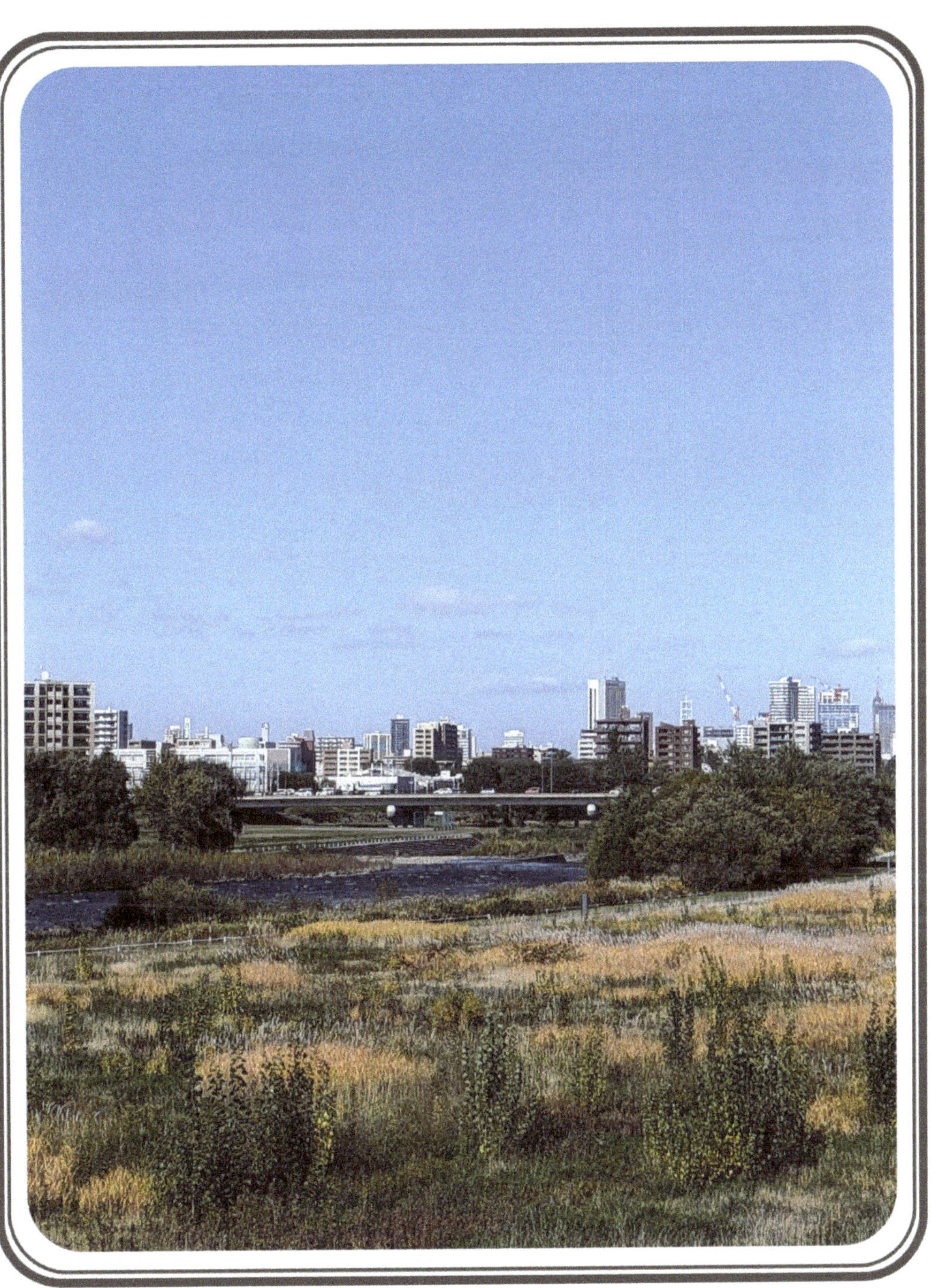

SILHOUETTE

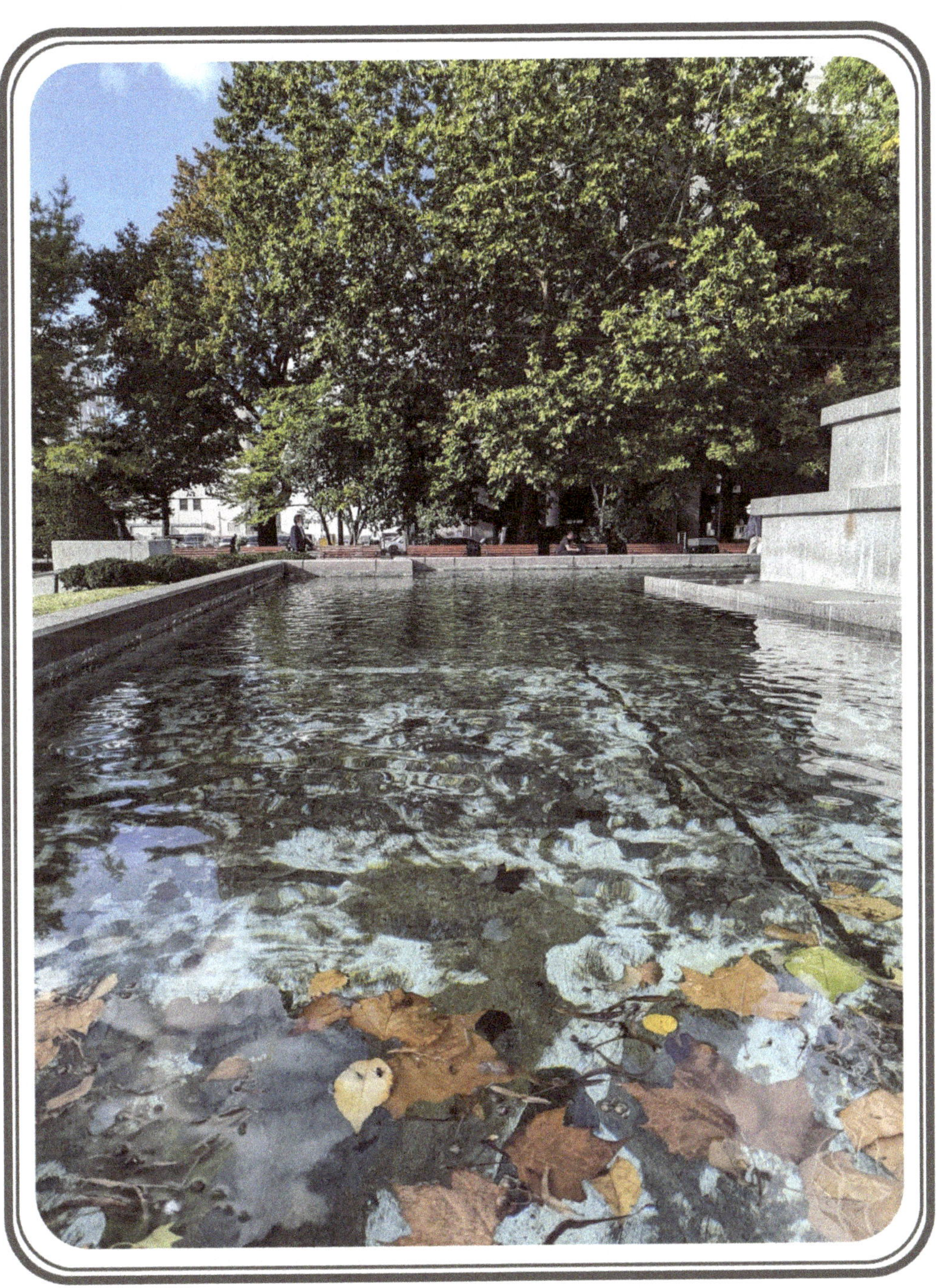

HARVEST

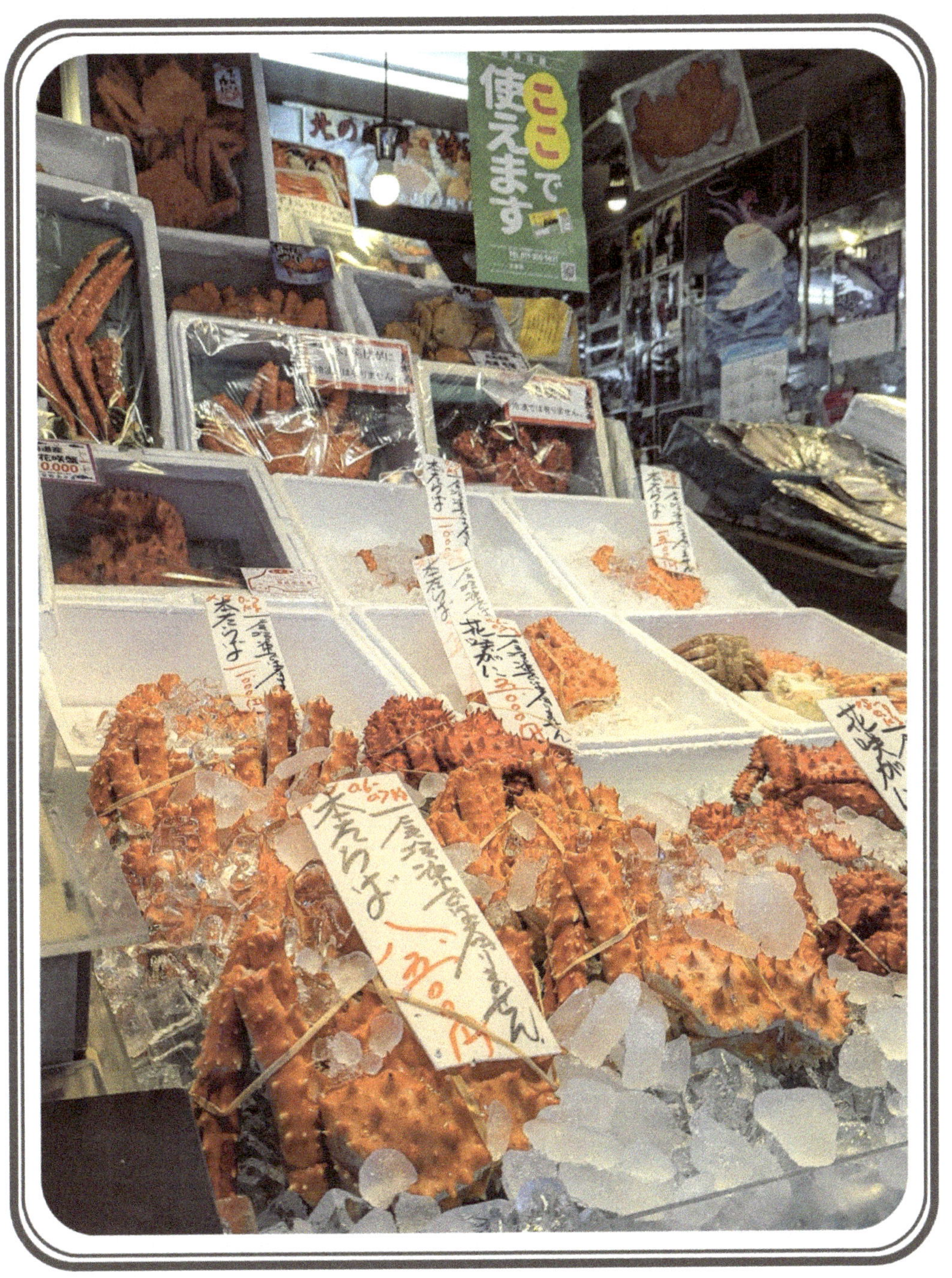
ここで使えます
本たらば
花咲がに

ORCHESTRINA

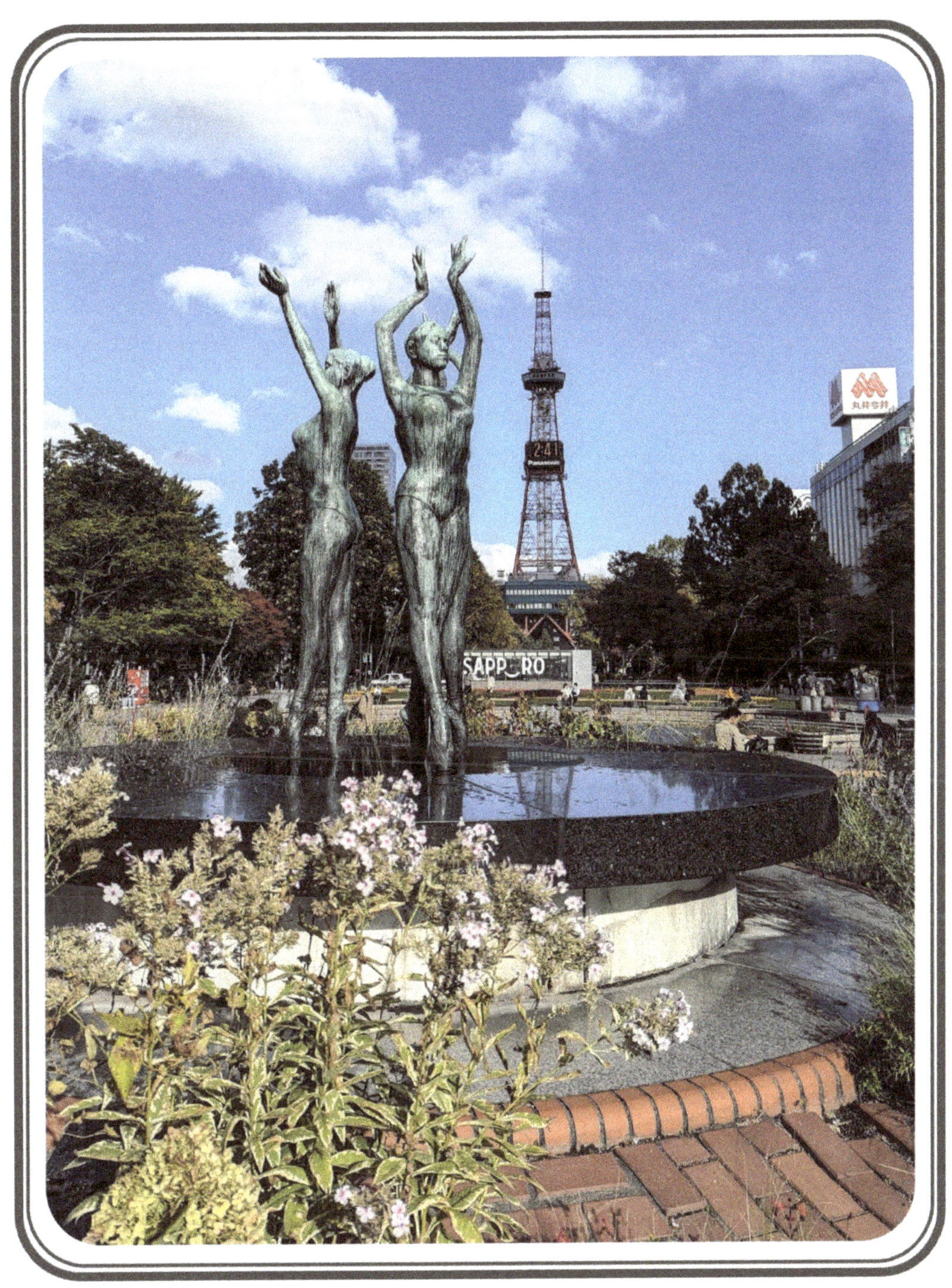
2:41
Panasonic
SAPPORO

BOUNCE

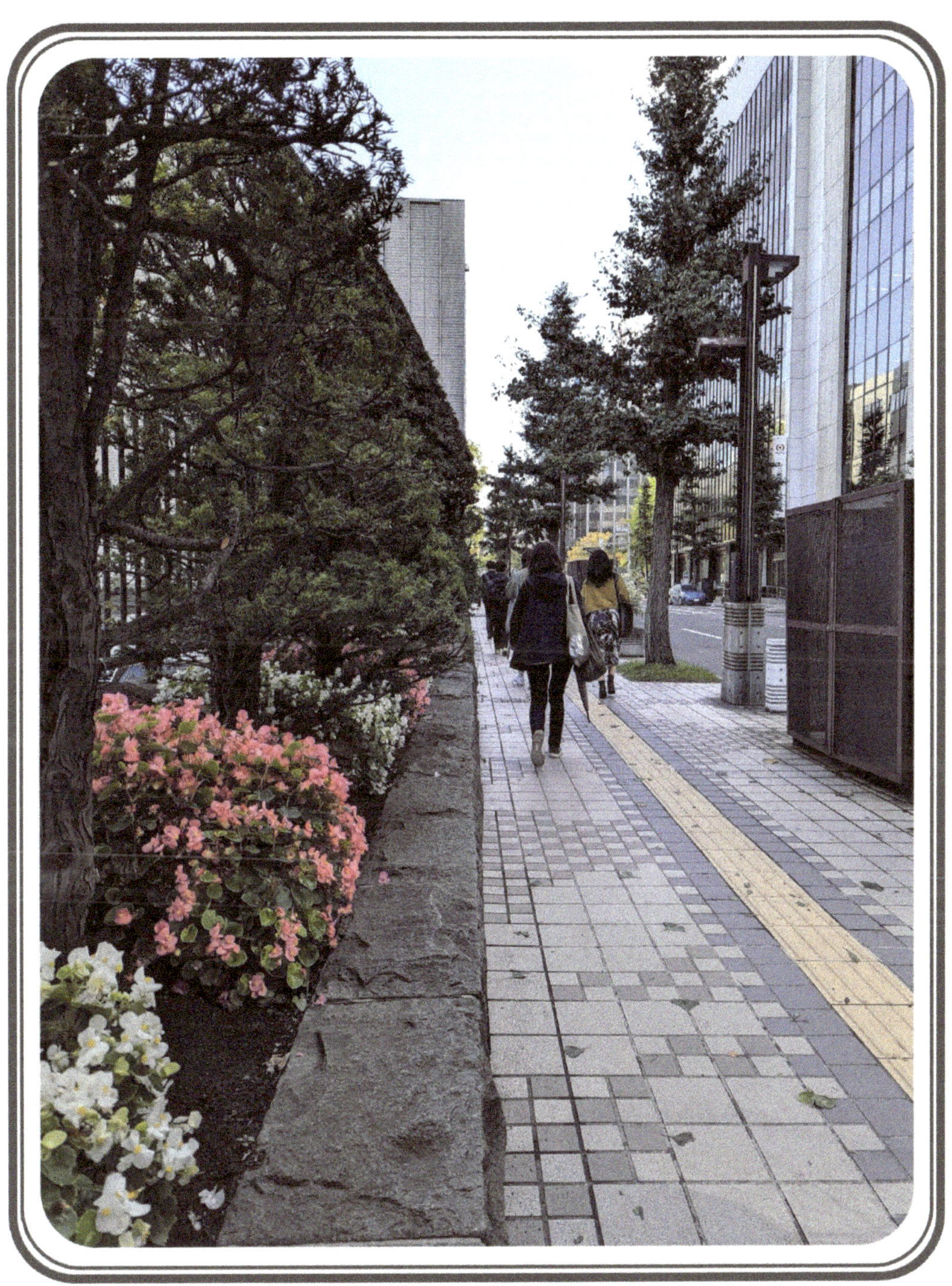

PROSPER

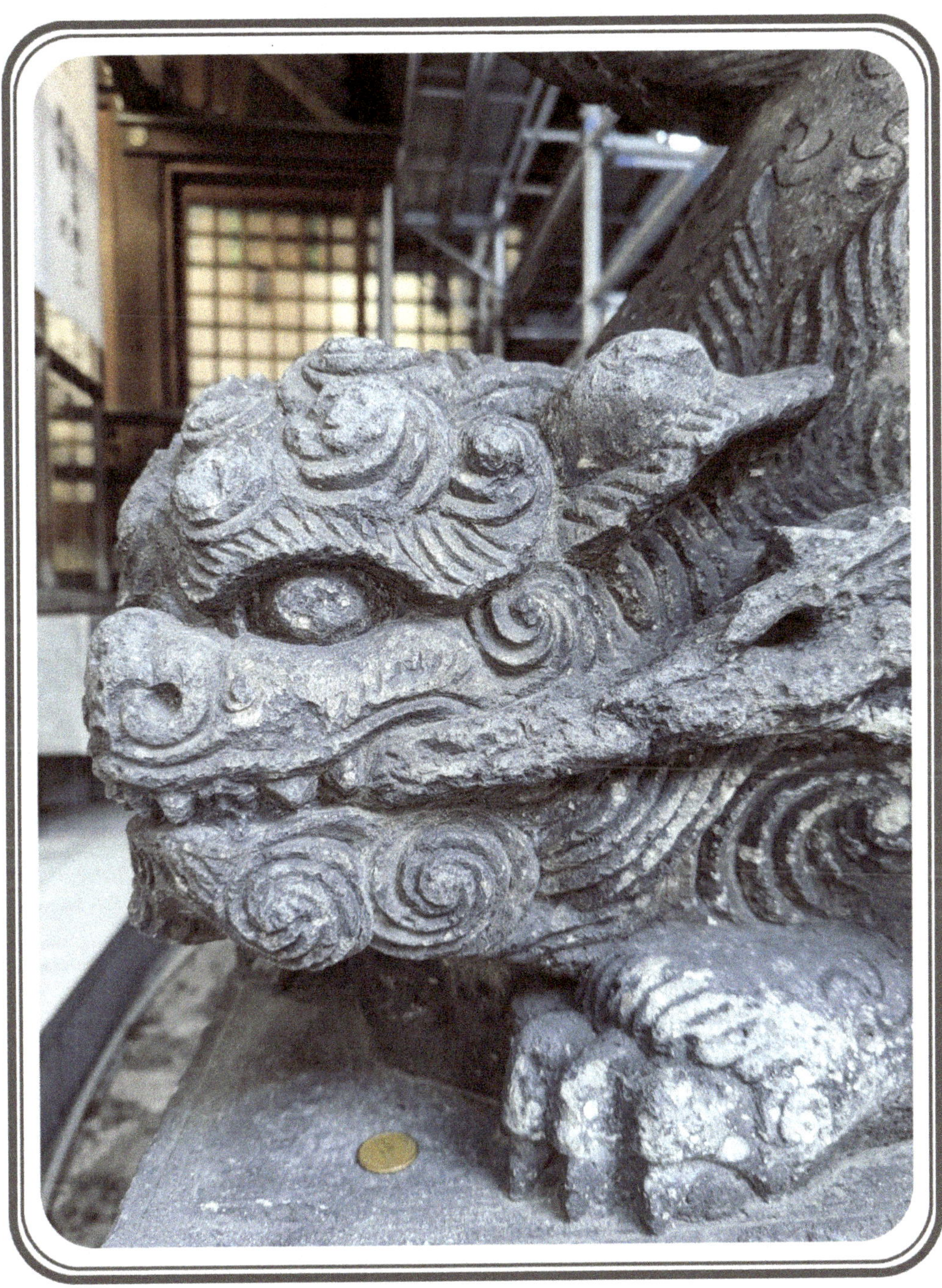

PLUGIN

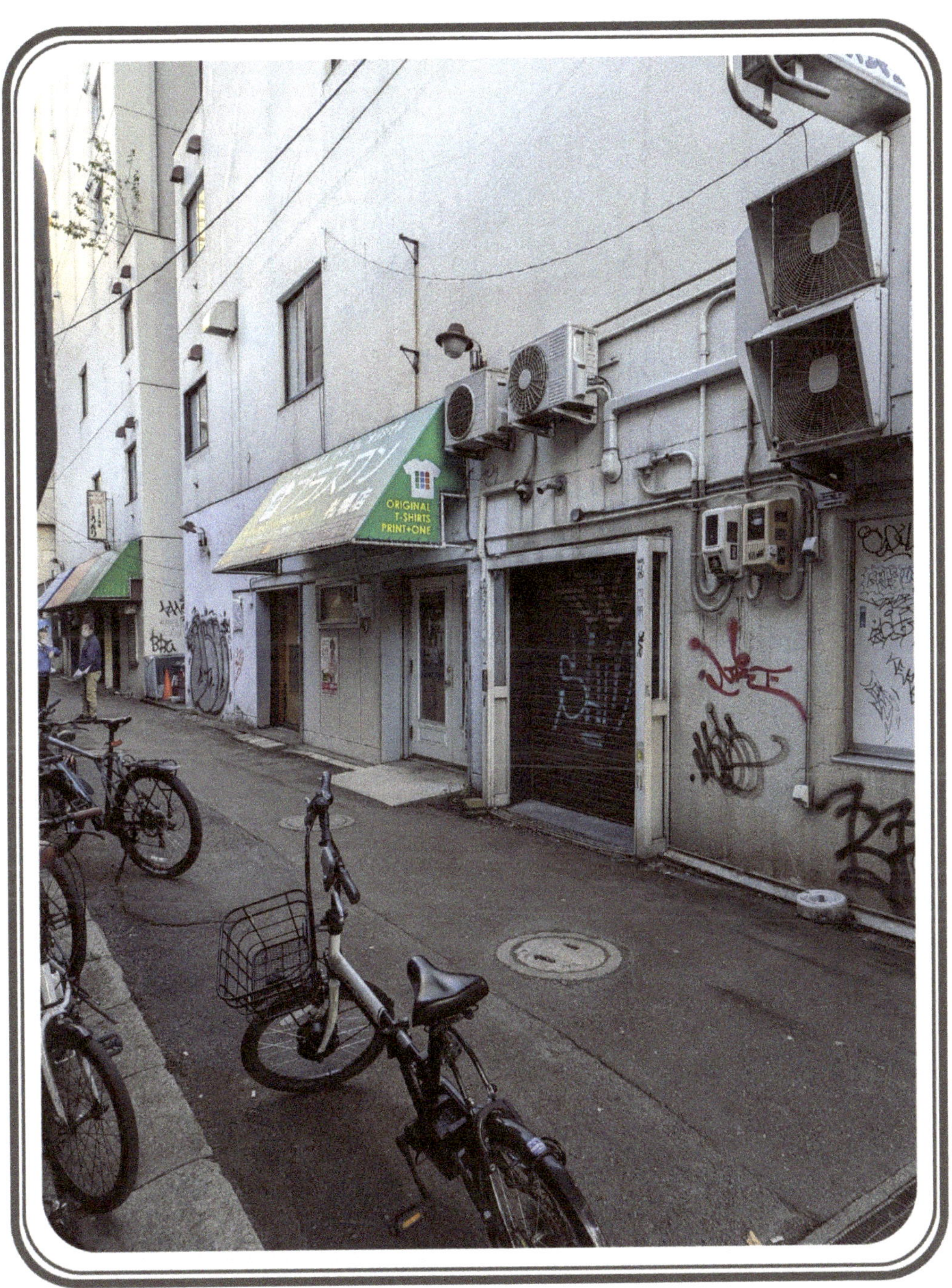
ORIGINAL
T-SHIRTS
PRINT+ONE

WALLACE

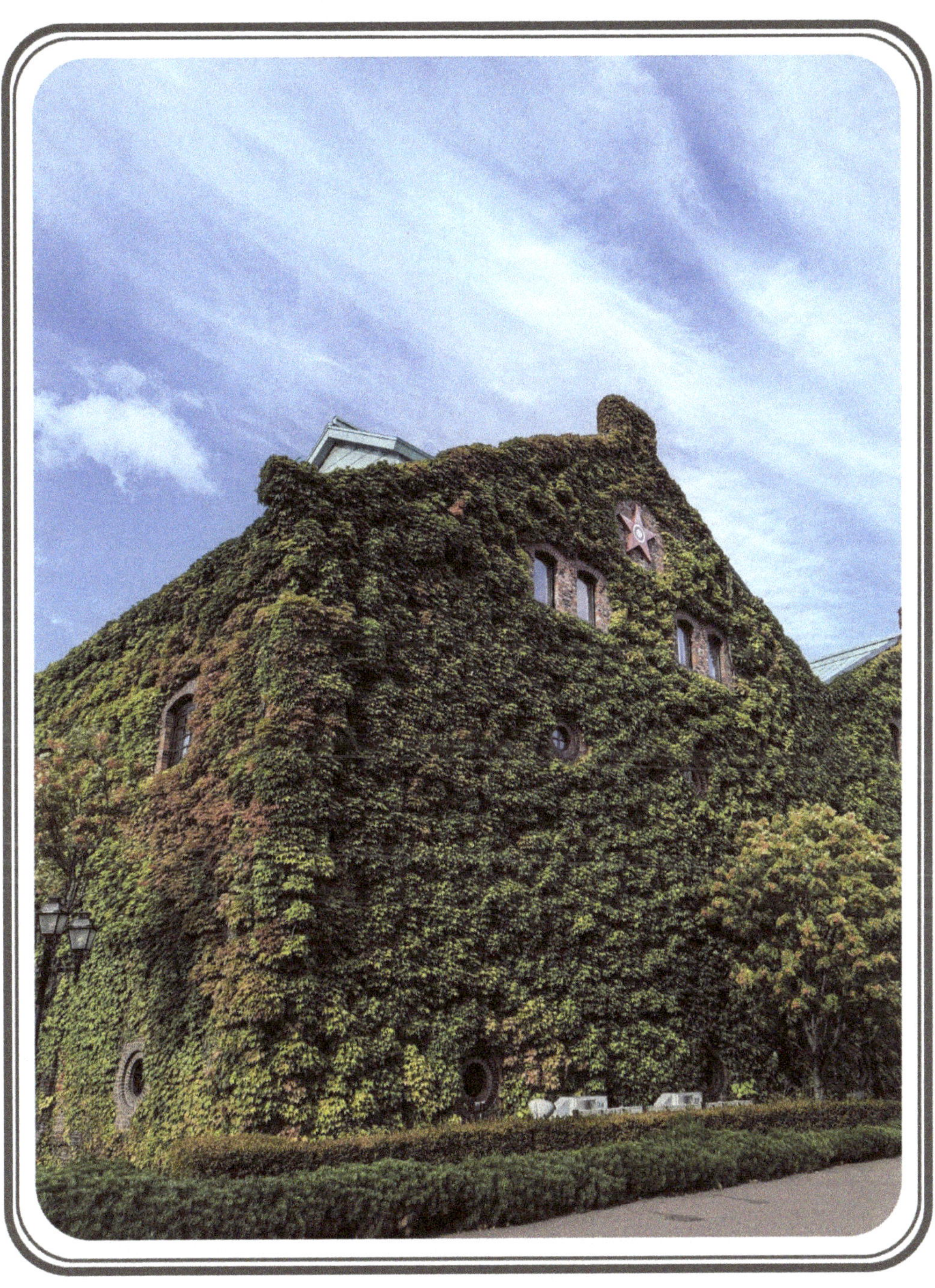

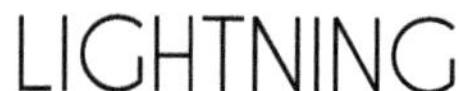

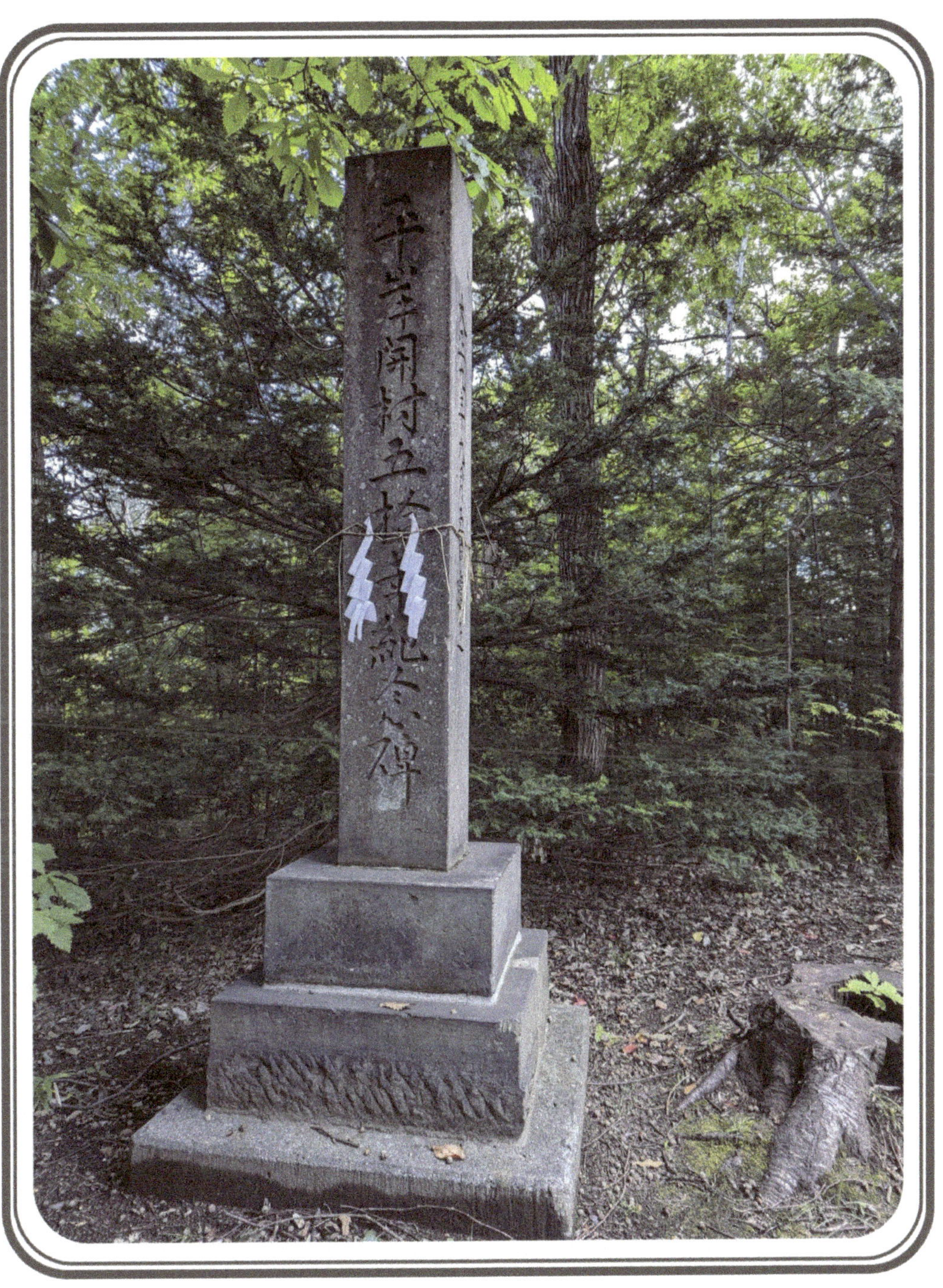
平岸開村五拾年紀念碑

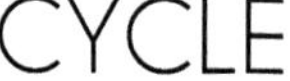
CYCLE

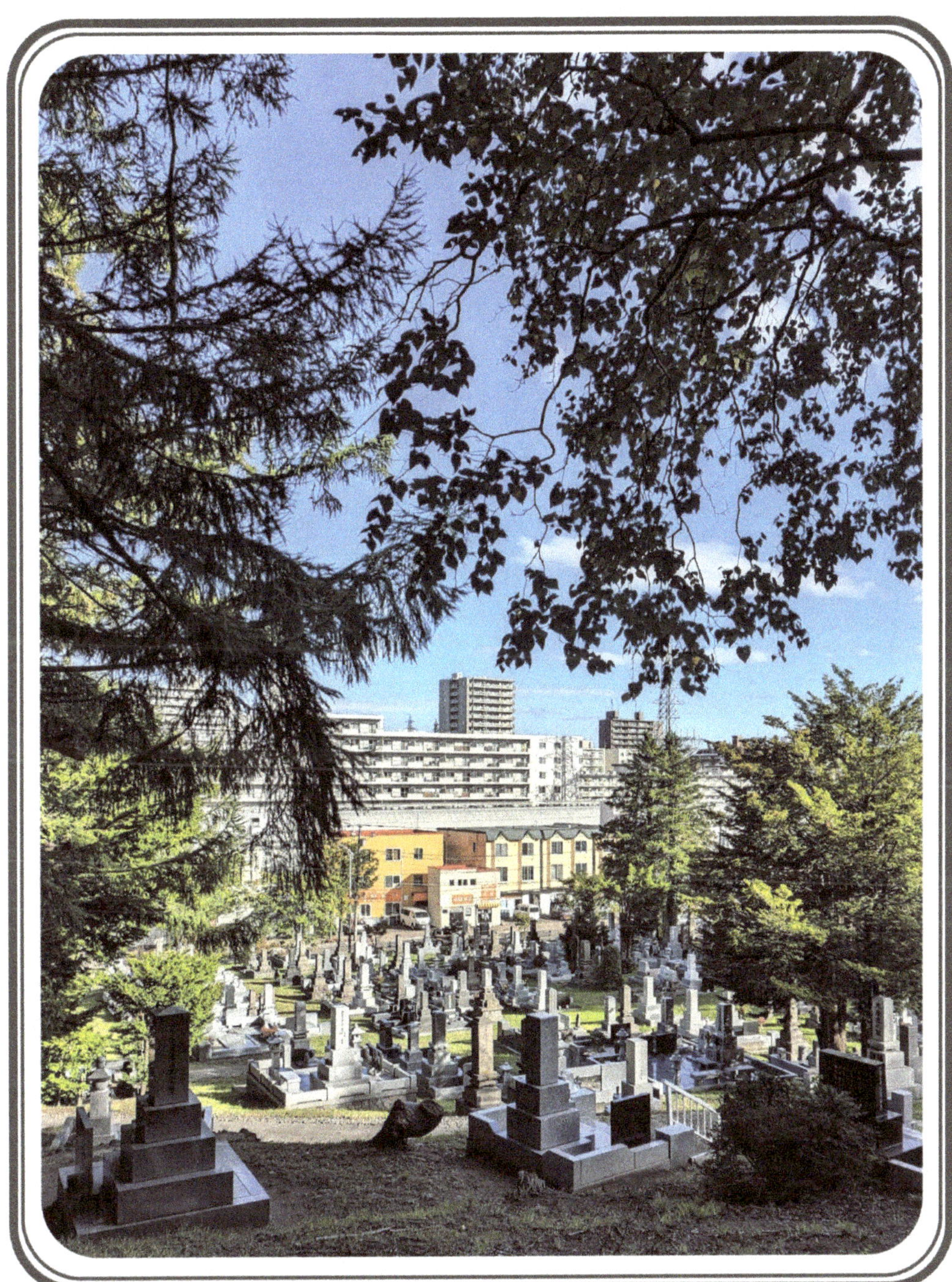

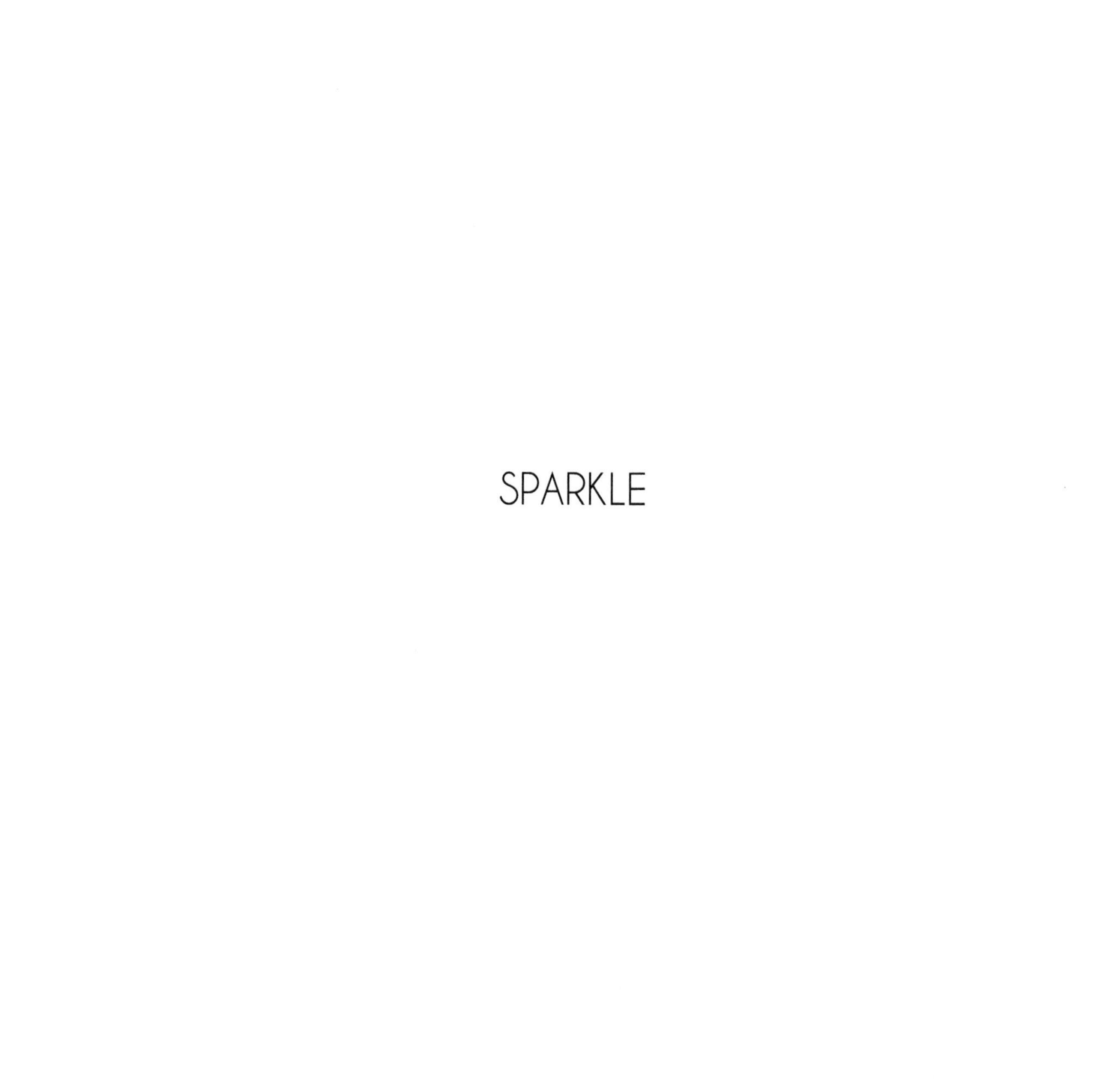

SPARKLE

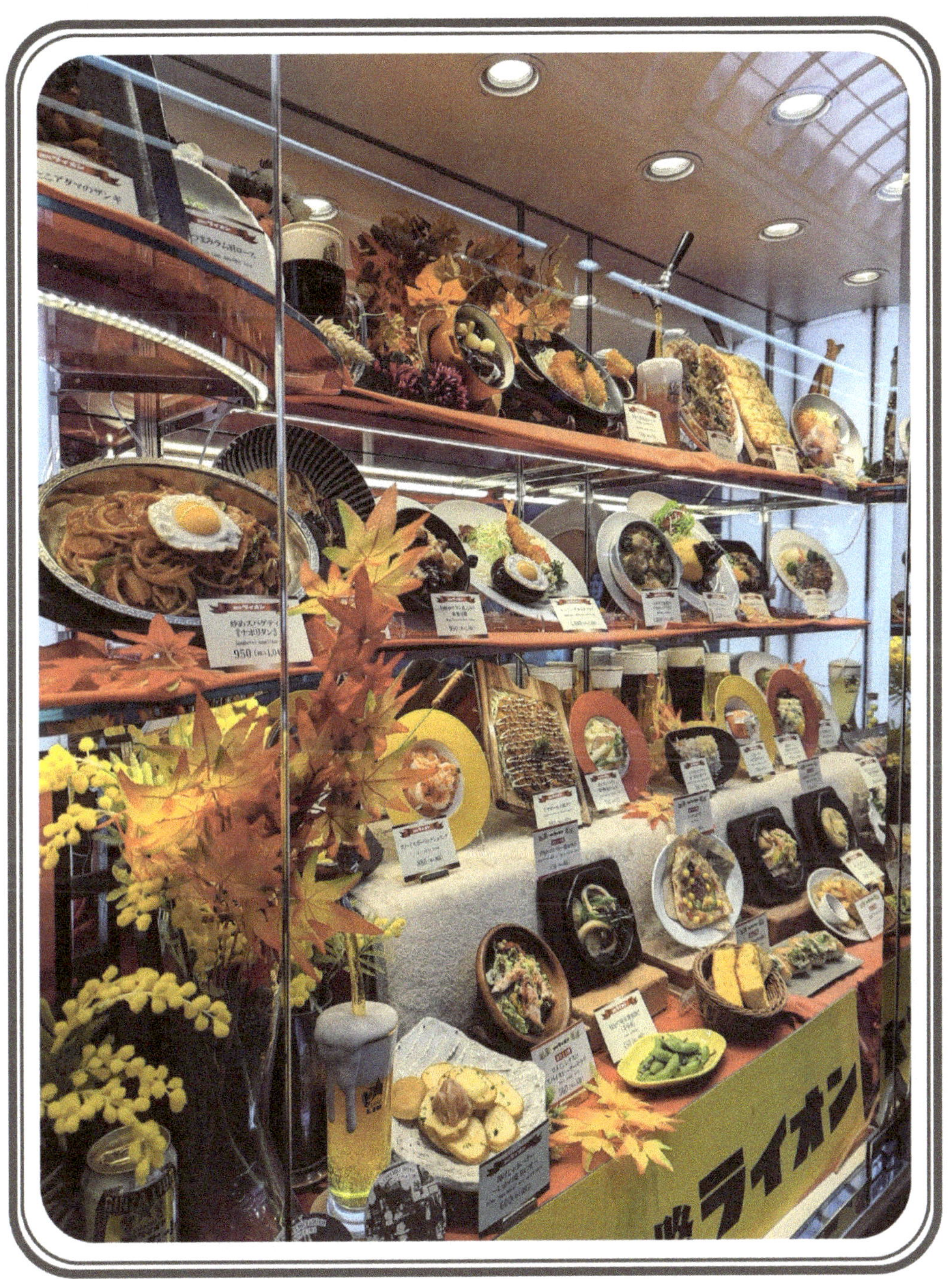
ライオン

SWEEP

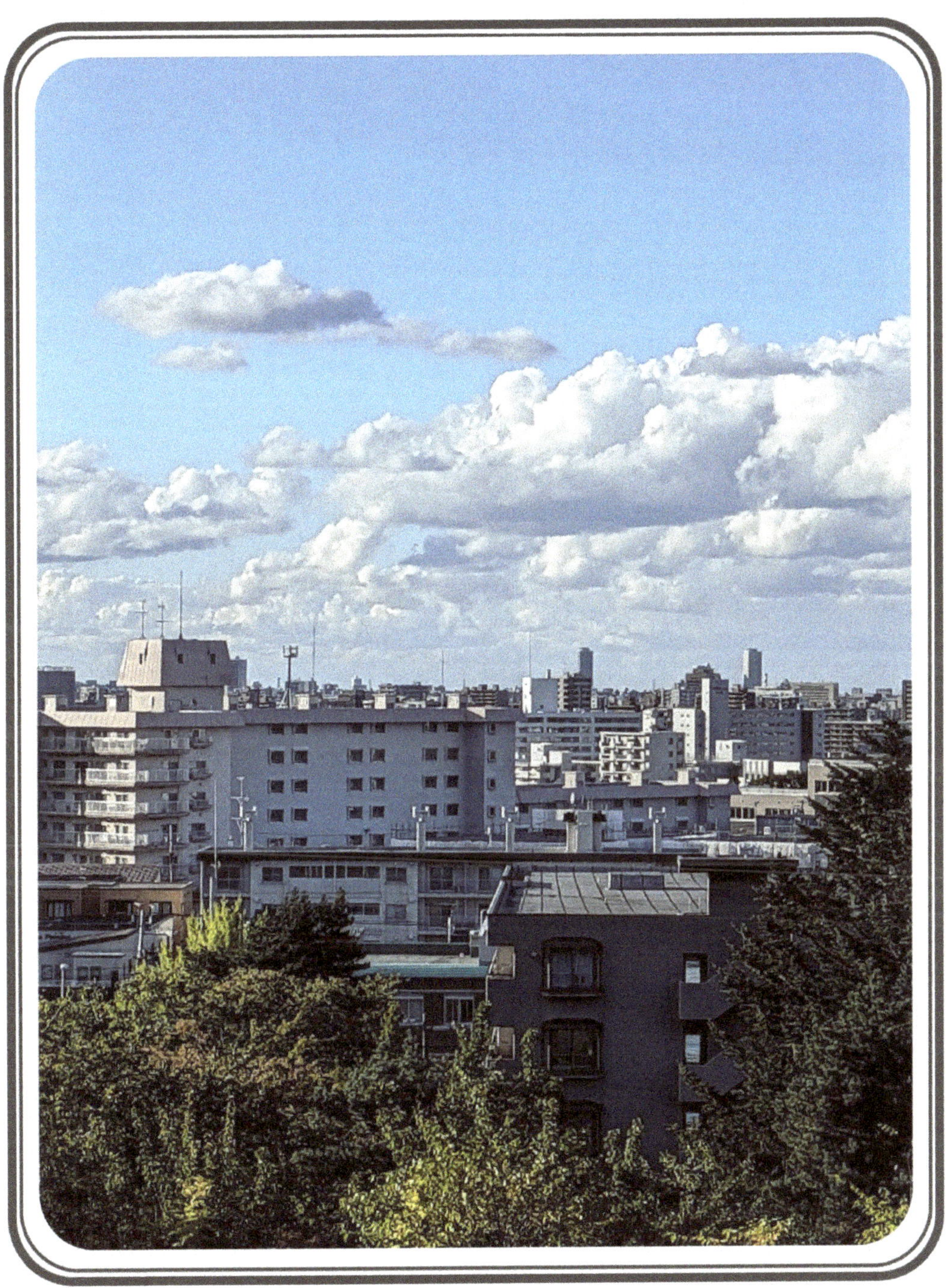

CANYON

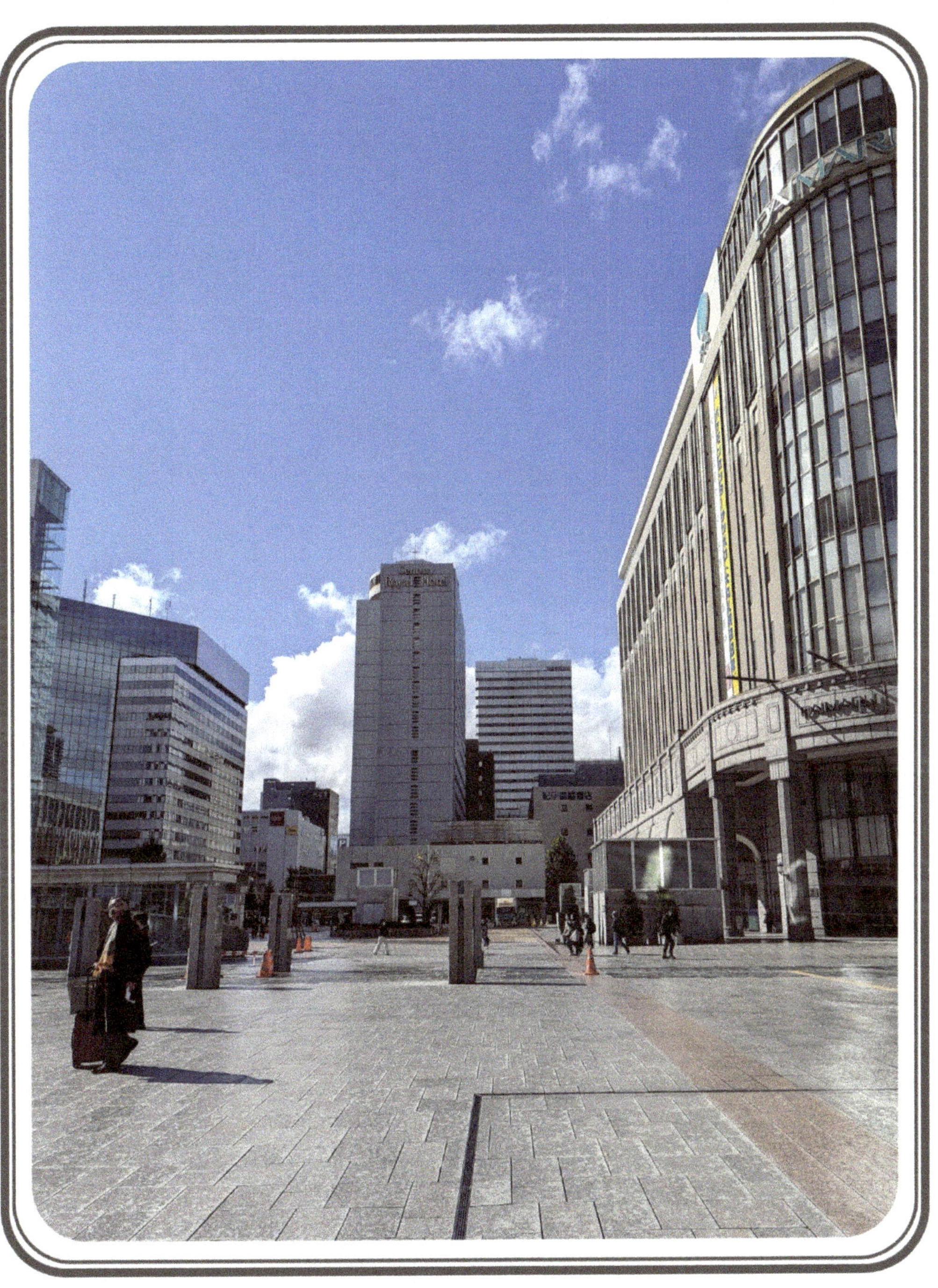

CYCLOPEAN

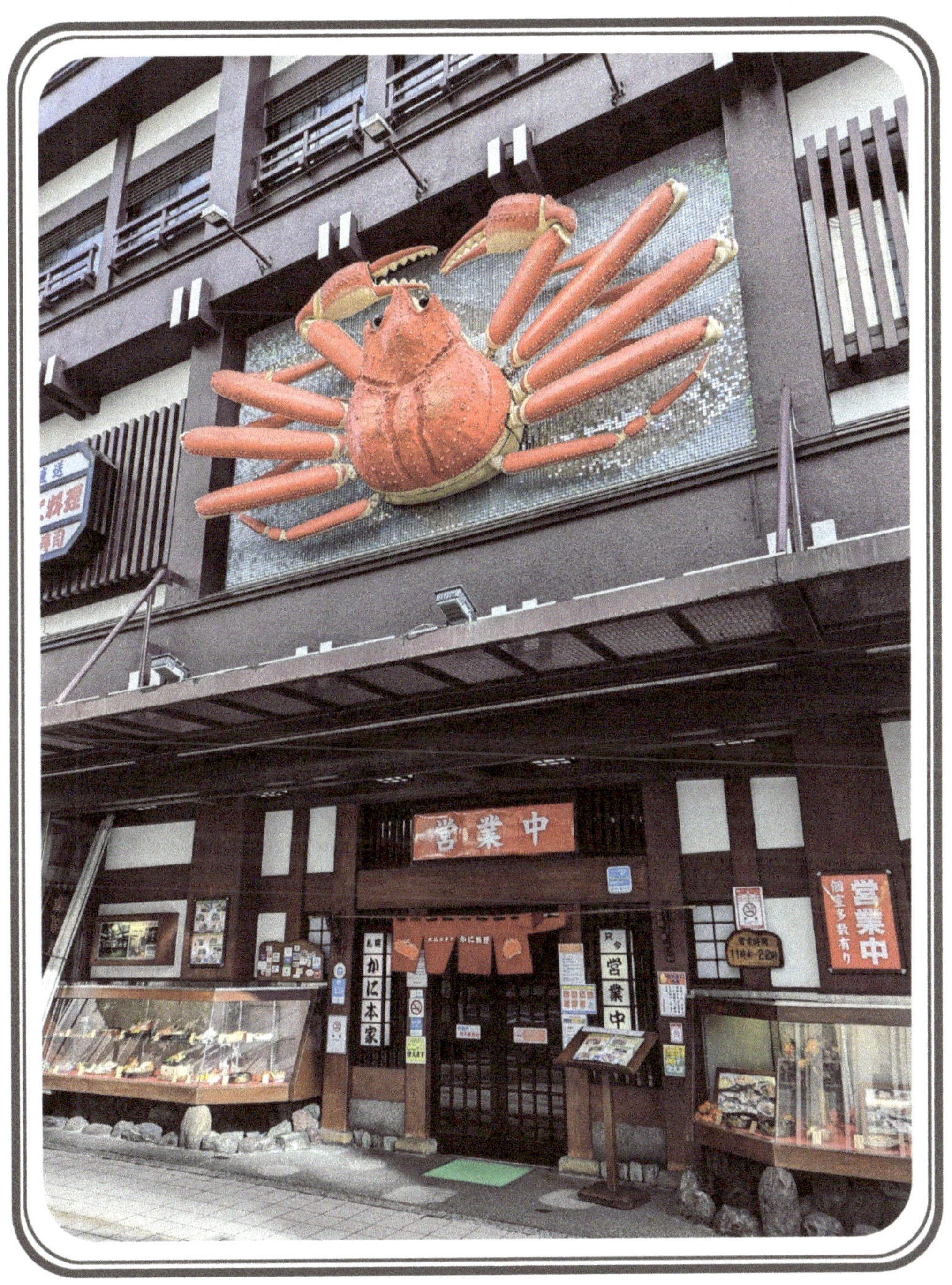
営業中
かに本家
只今
営業中
営業中
個室多数有り

ESCHER

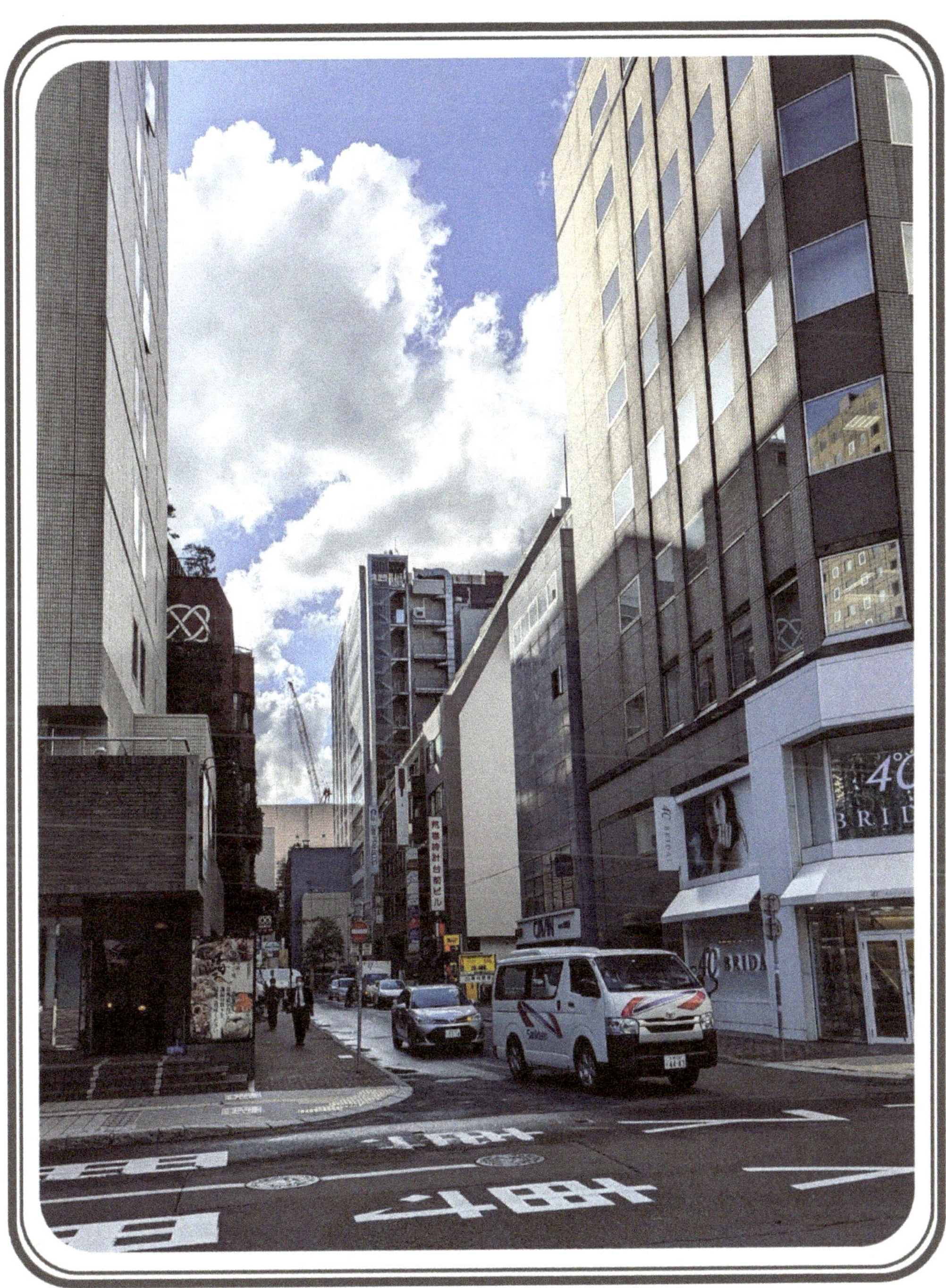
4℃
BRID
4℃ BRIDA

SLIPSTREAM

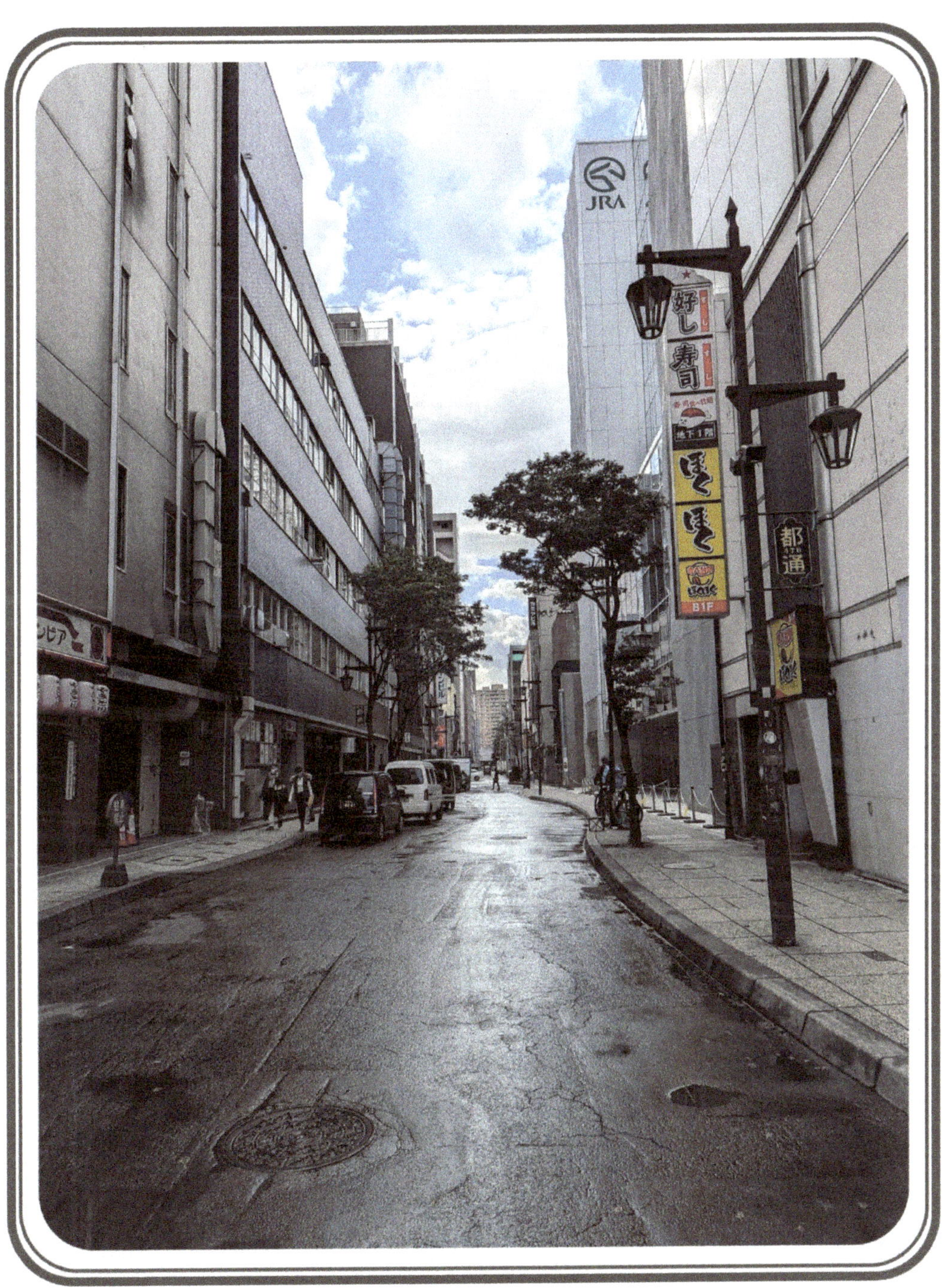
JRA
好し寿司
ほくほく
B1F
都通

SOVEREIGN

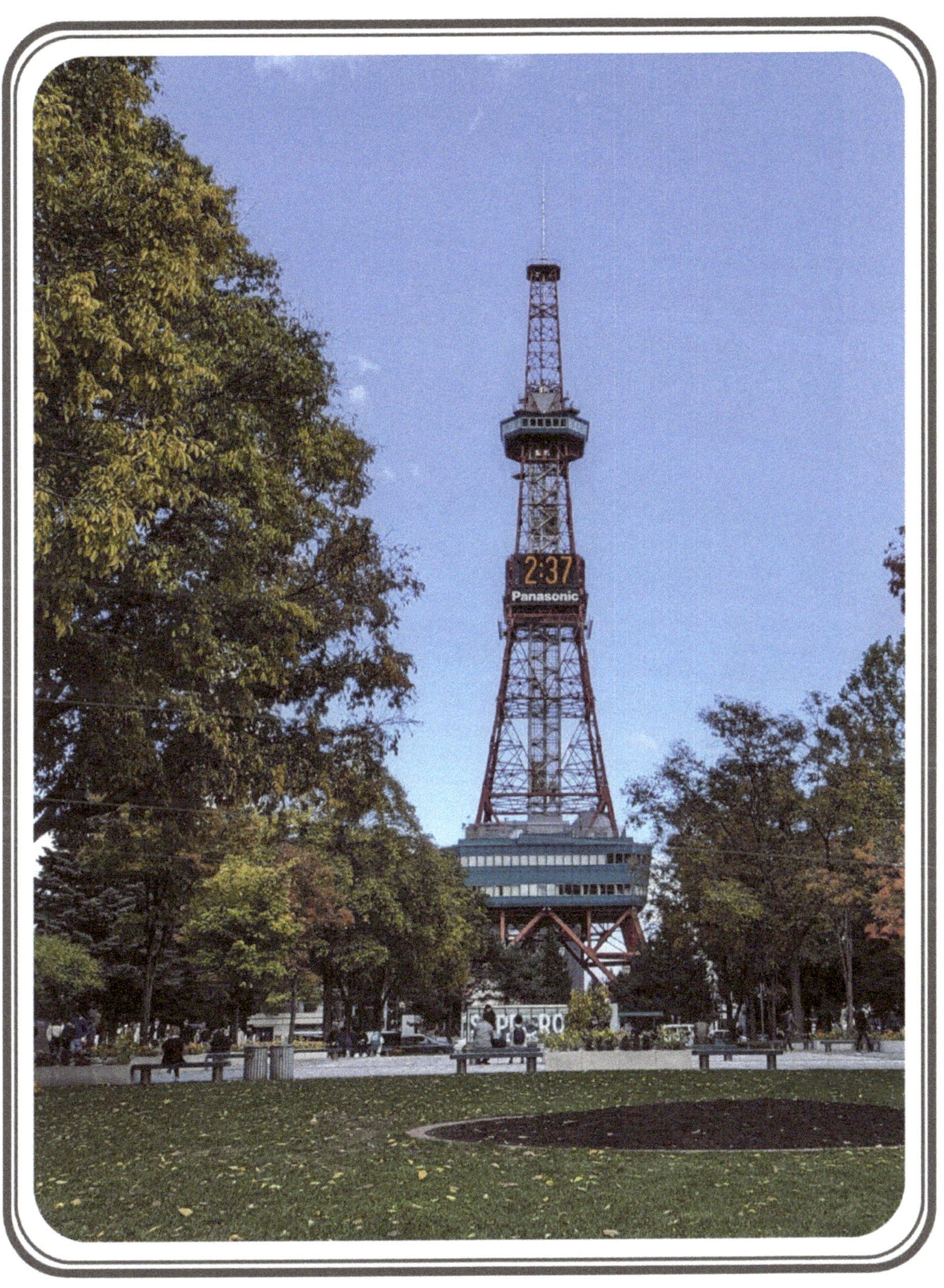
2:37
Panasonic

COVE

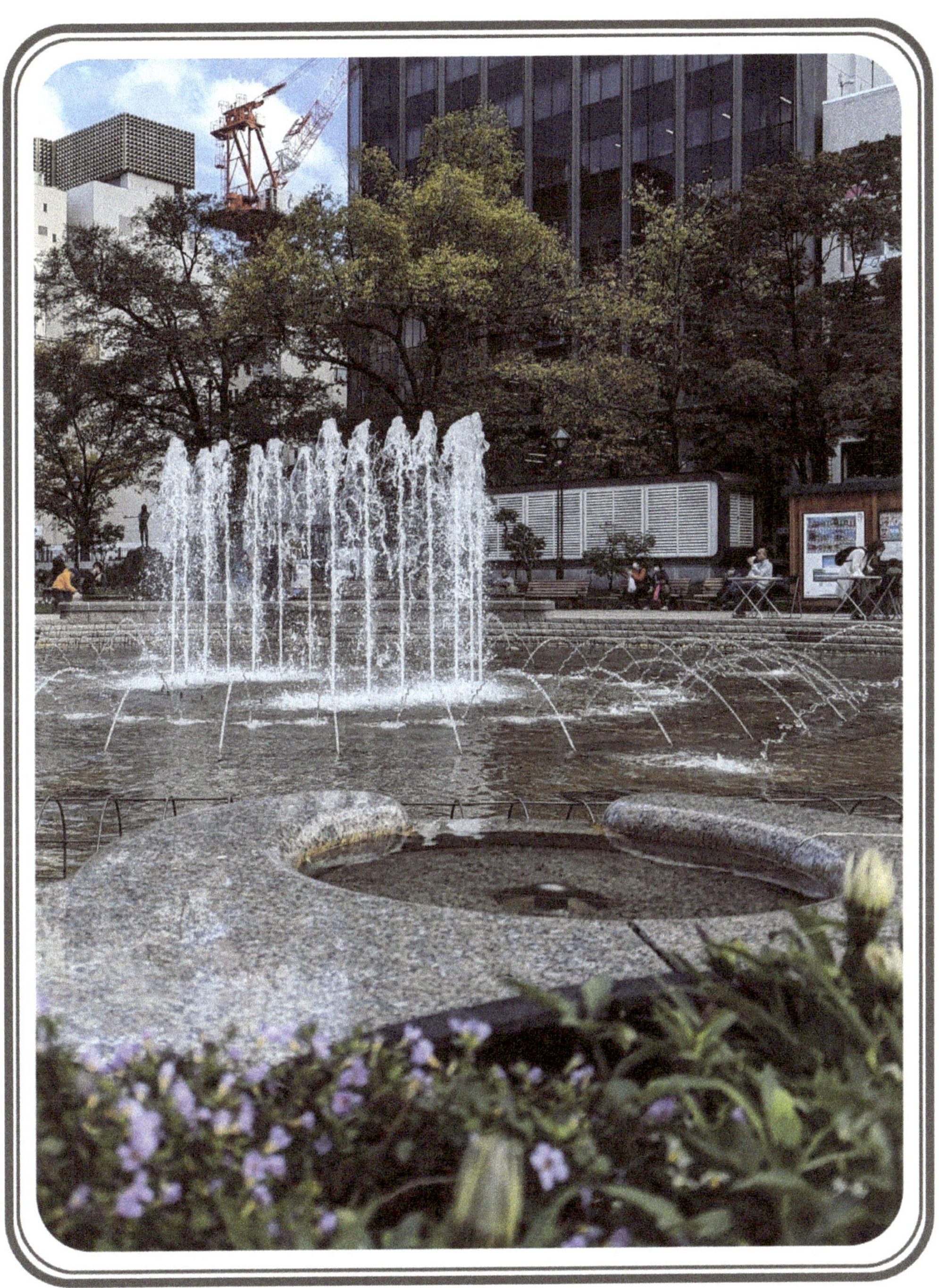

PONDER

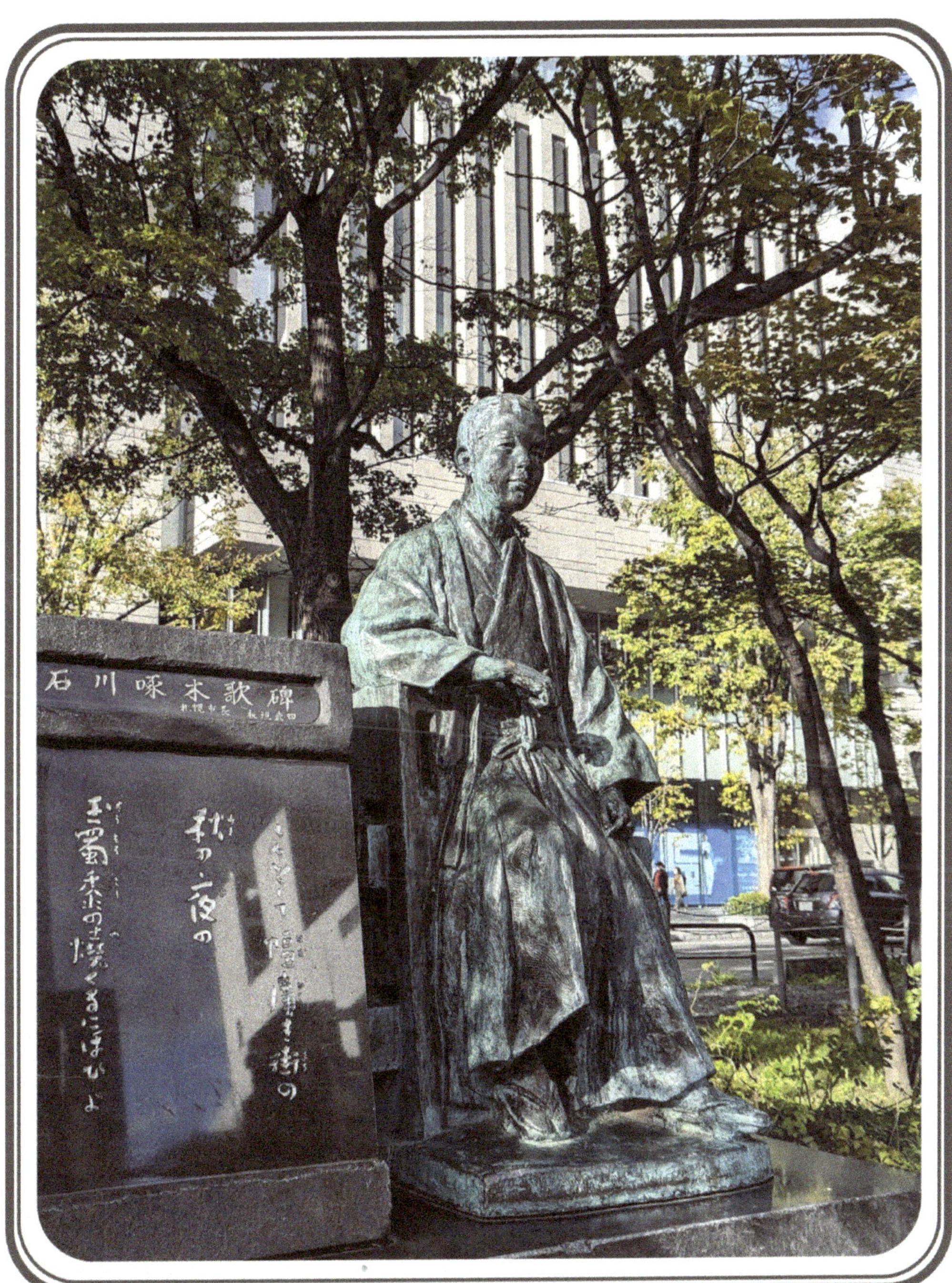
石川啄木歌碑
秋の夜の
玉蜀黍の焼くるにほひよ

COMPASS

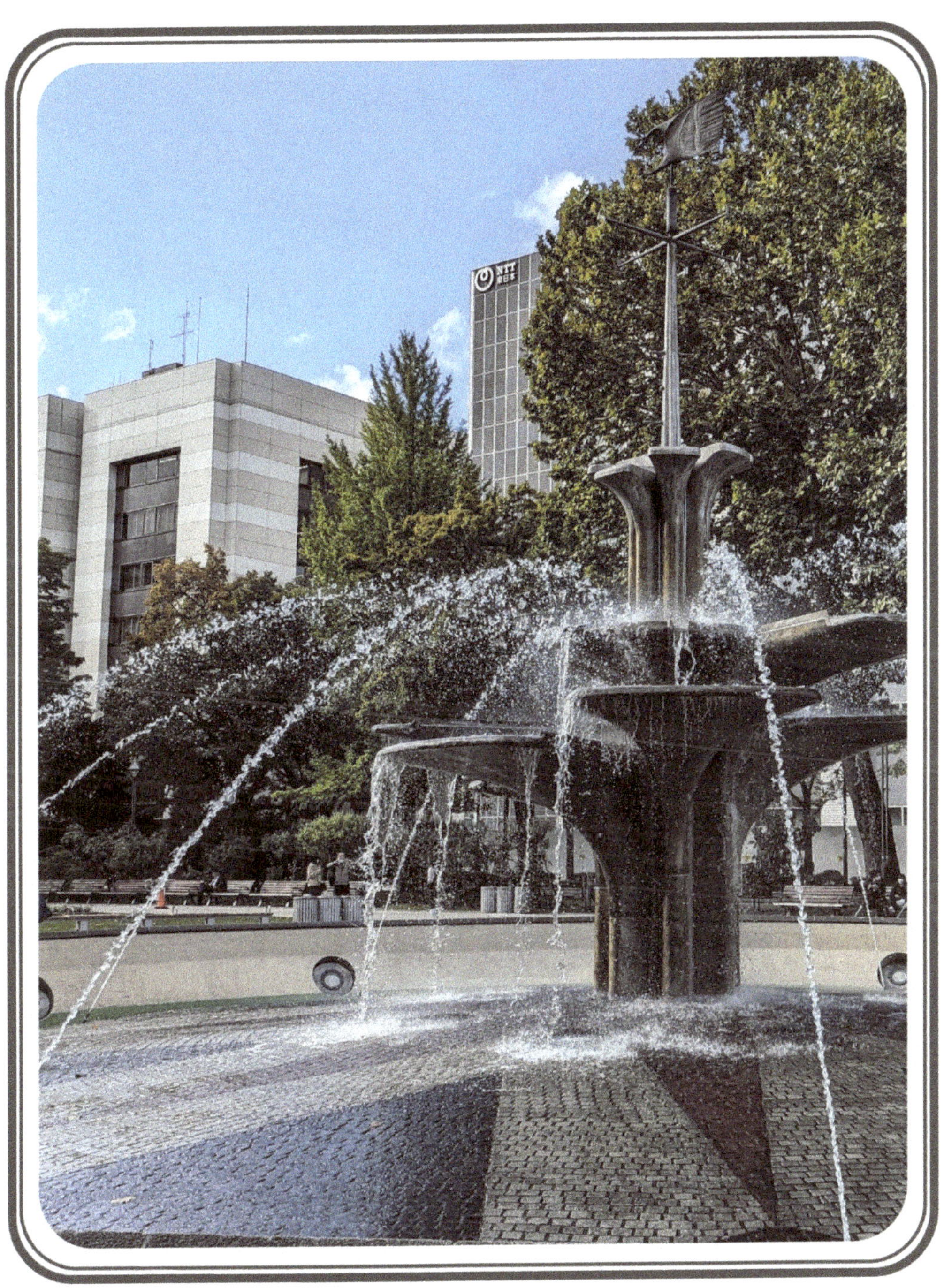
NTT

SARMAK

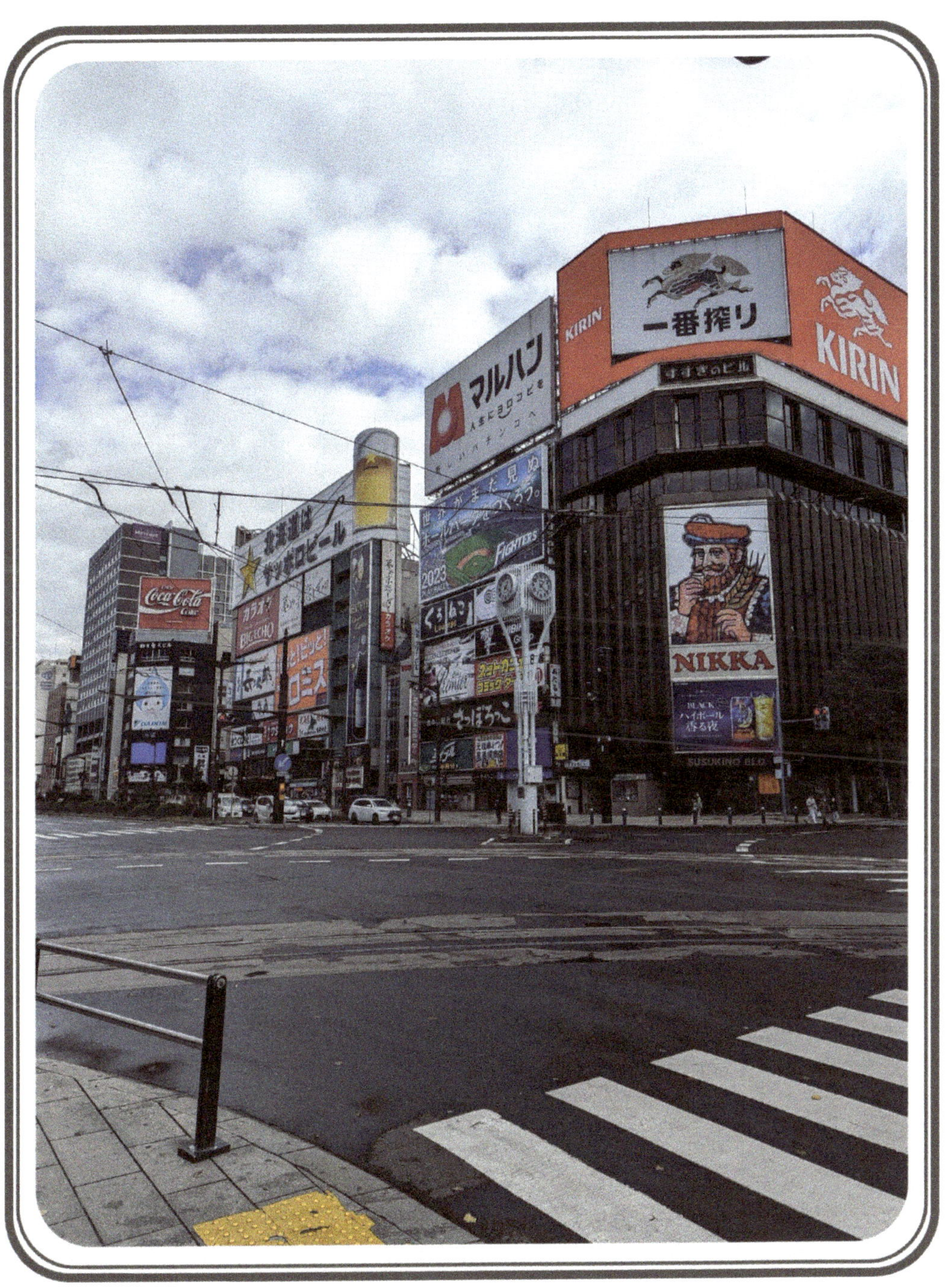

KIRIN
一番搾り
KIRIN
すすきのビル
マルハン
北海道は
サッポロビール
Coca-Cola
FIGHTERS
NIKKA

WAITING

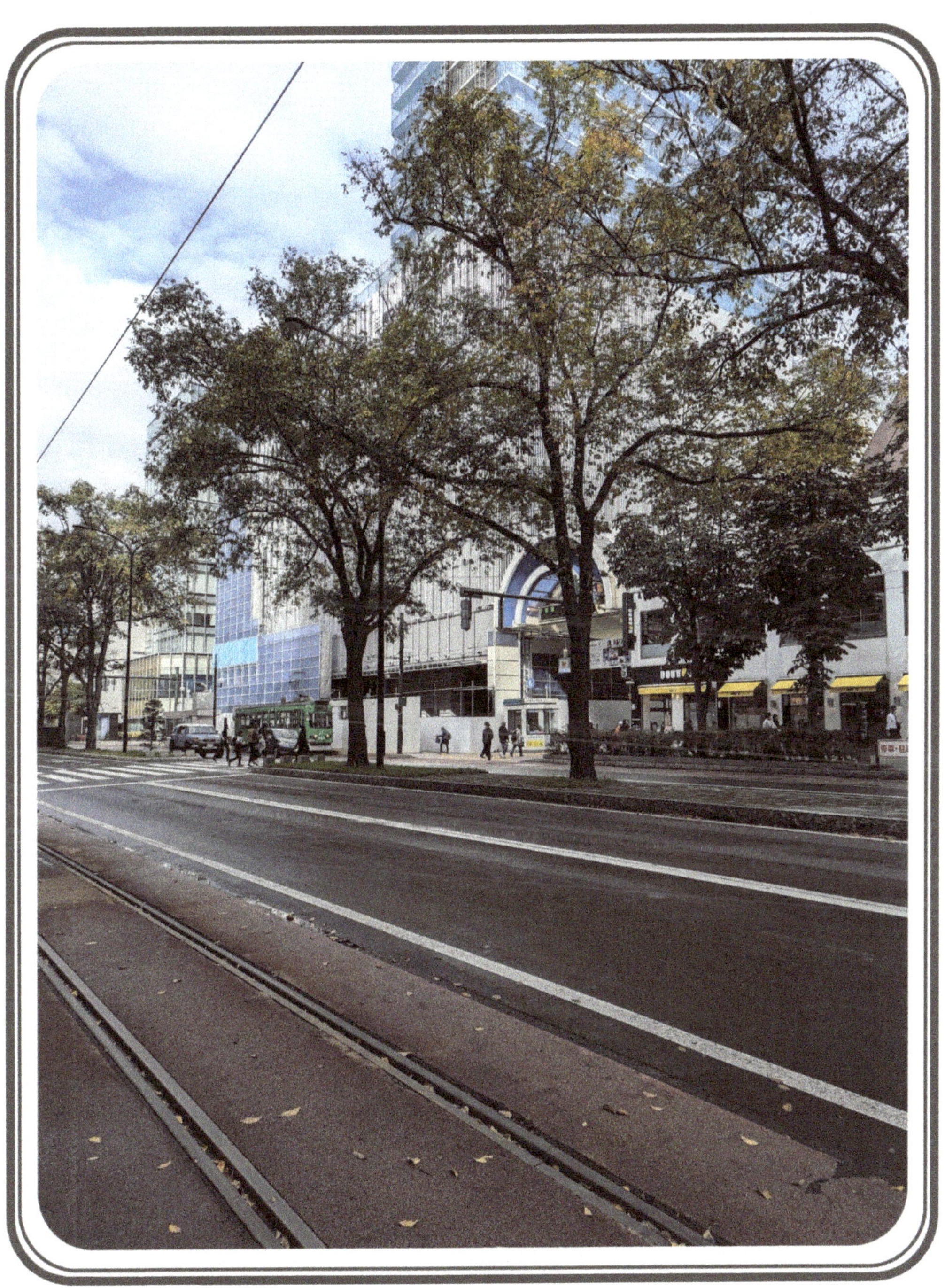

OFFERING

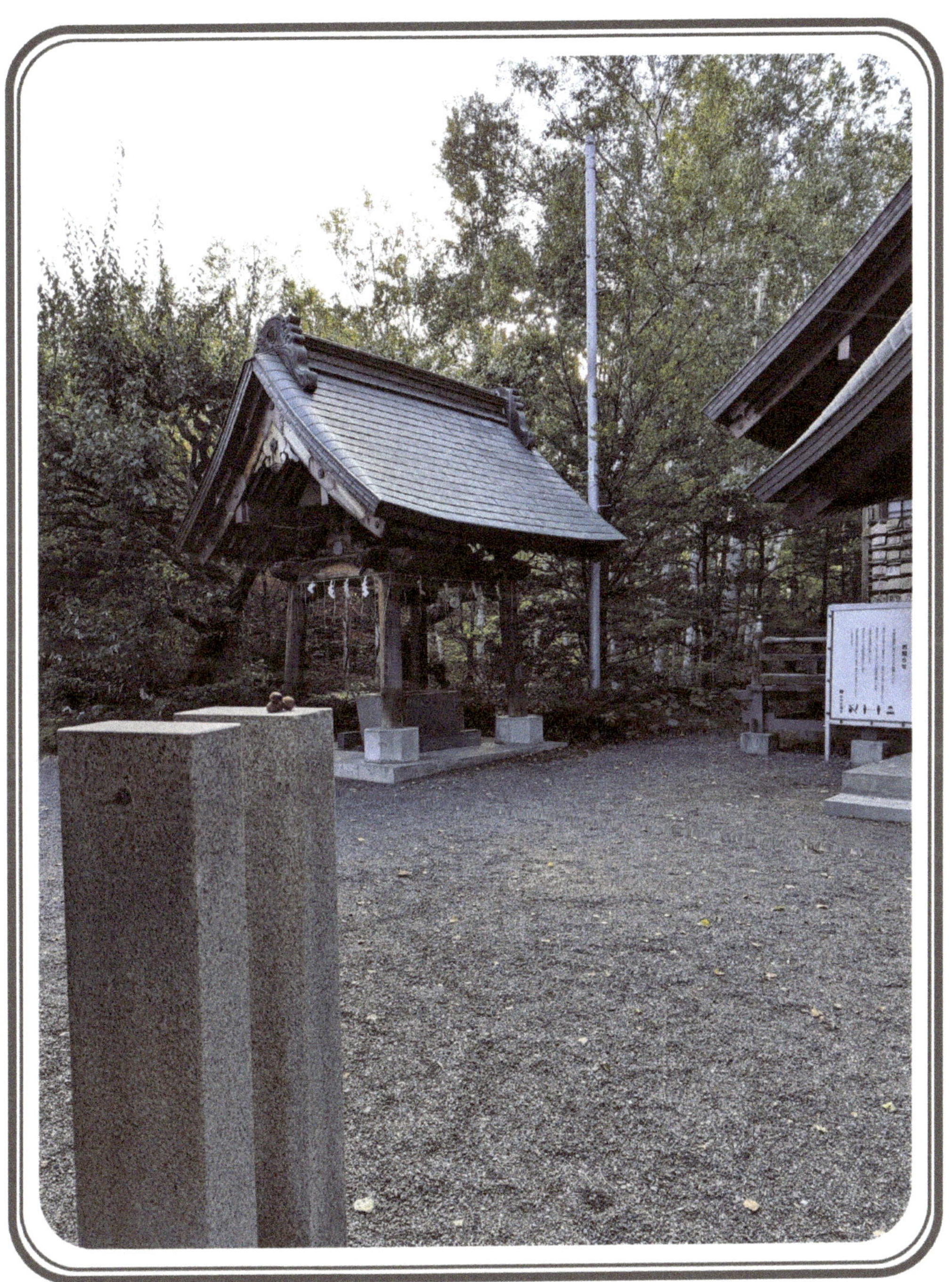

PELT

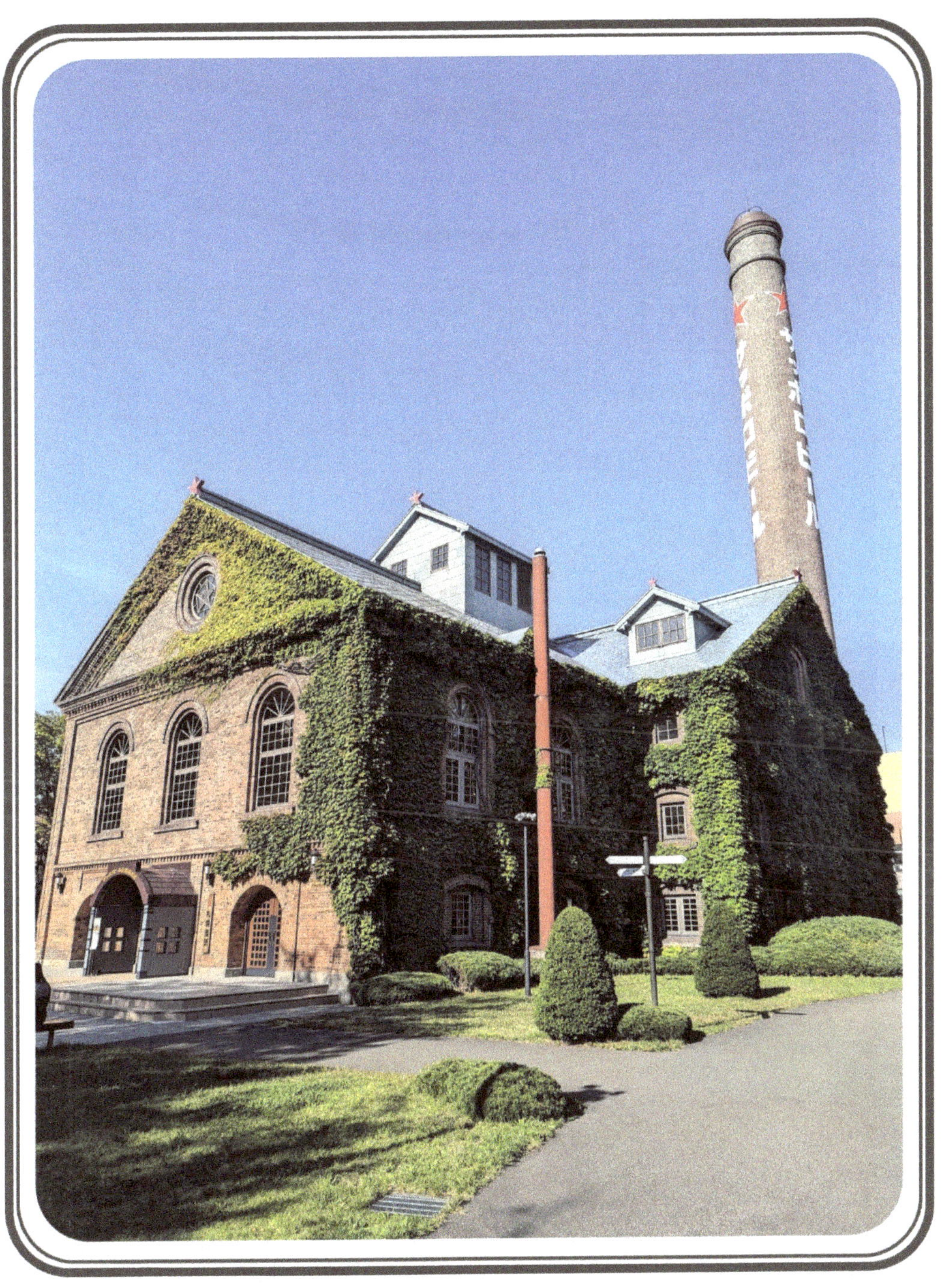
サッポロビール

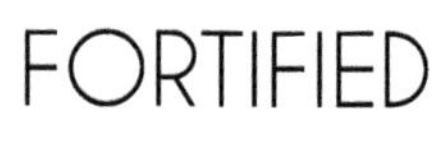
FORTIFIED

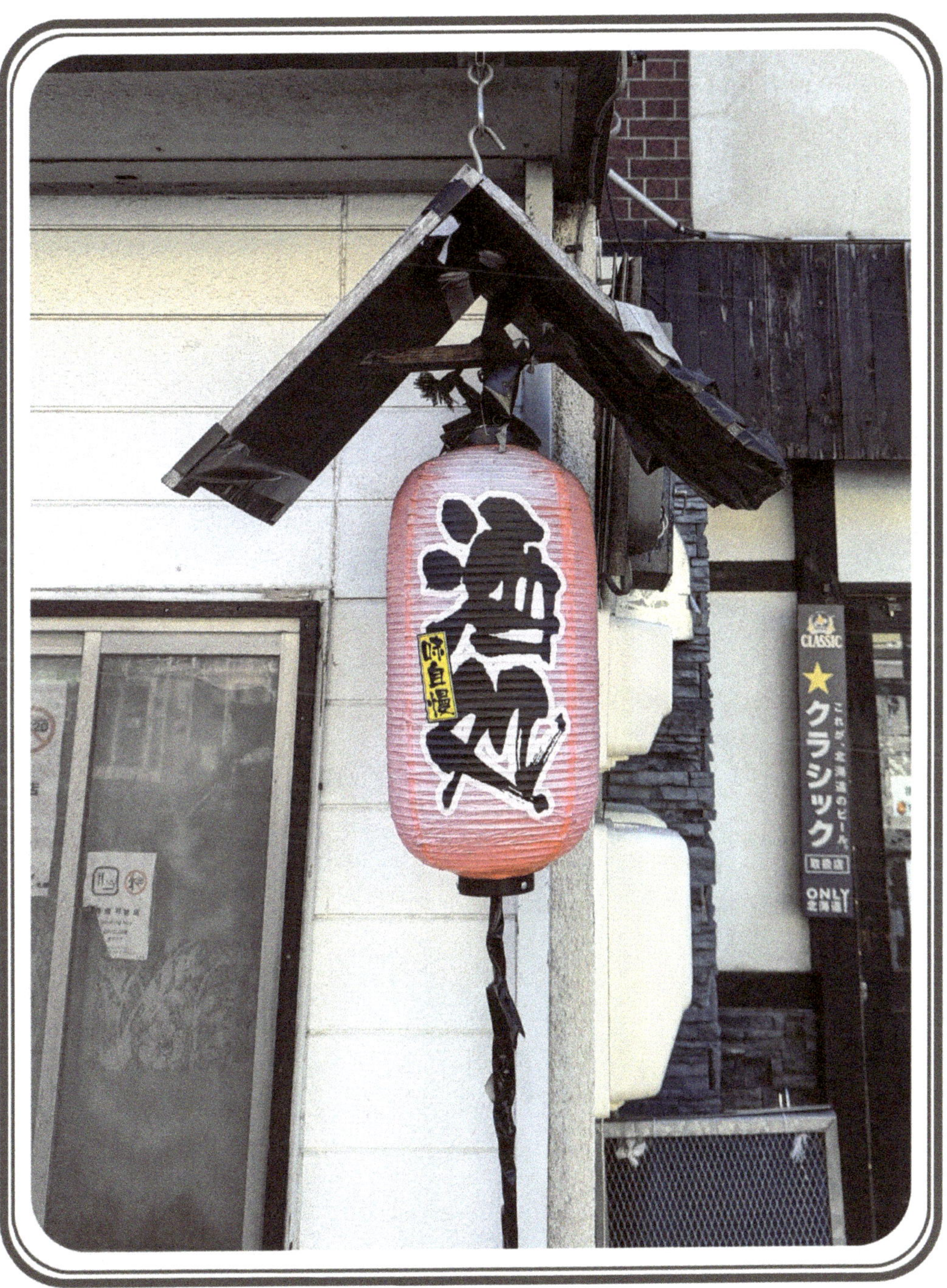
味自慢
CLASSIC
クラシック
ONLY

OVERLOOK

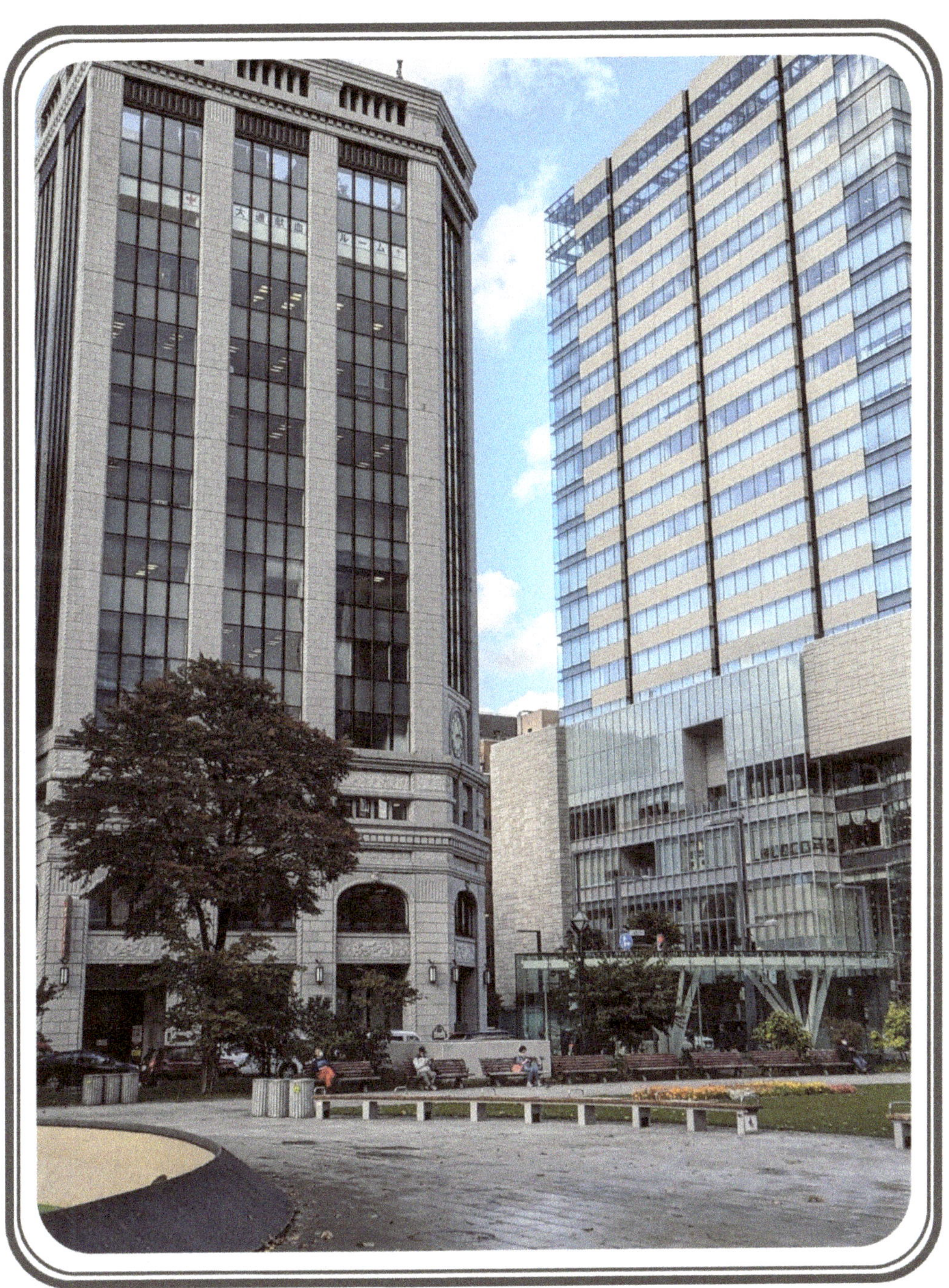
大通献血
ルーム

UNDERSEA

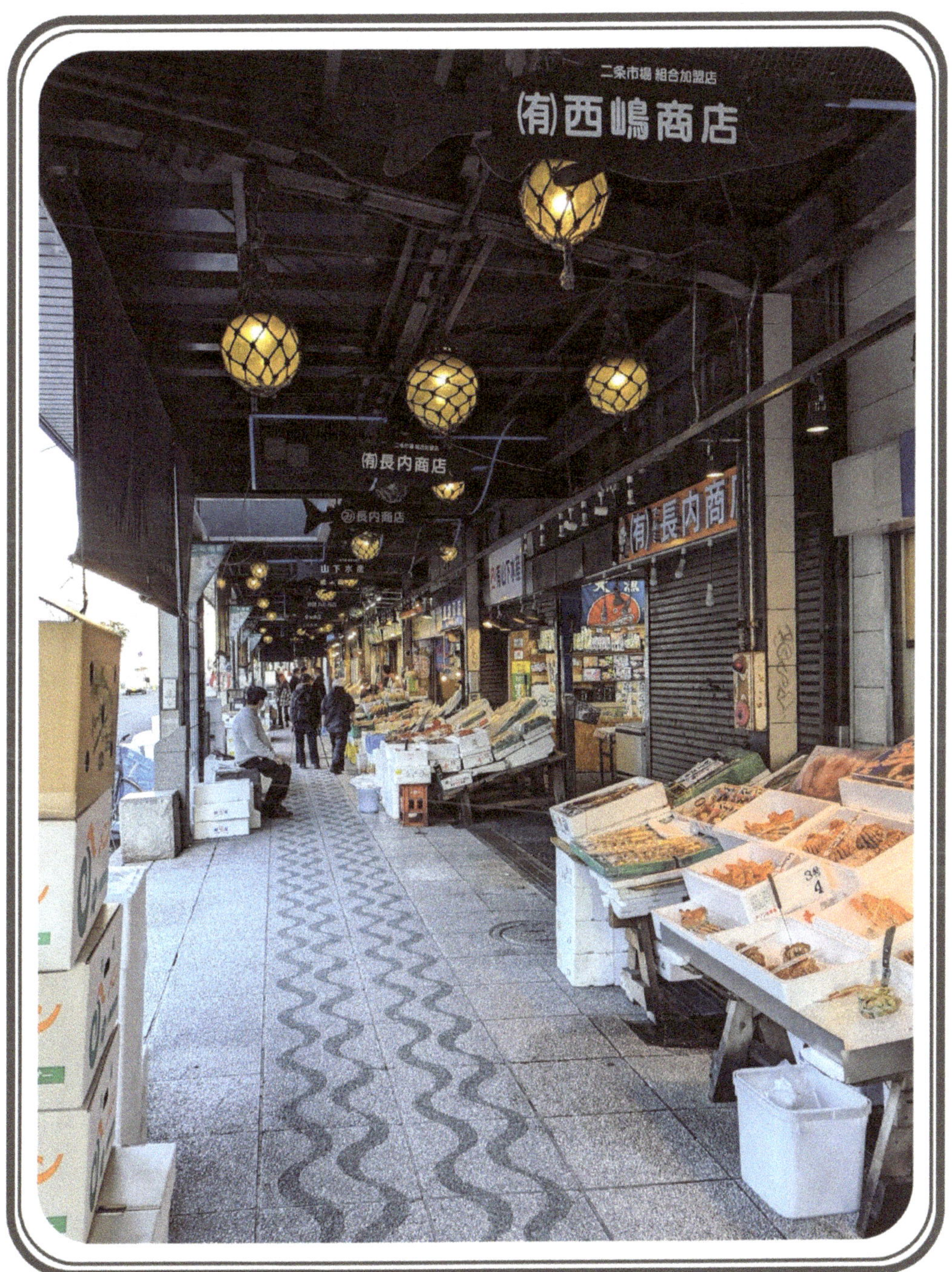

二条市場 組合加盟店
㈲西嶋商店
㈲長内商店
山下水産

SUBMARINE

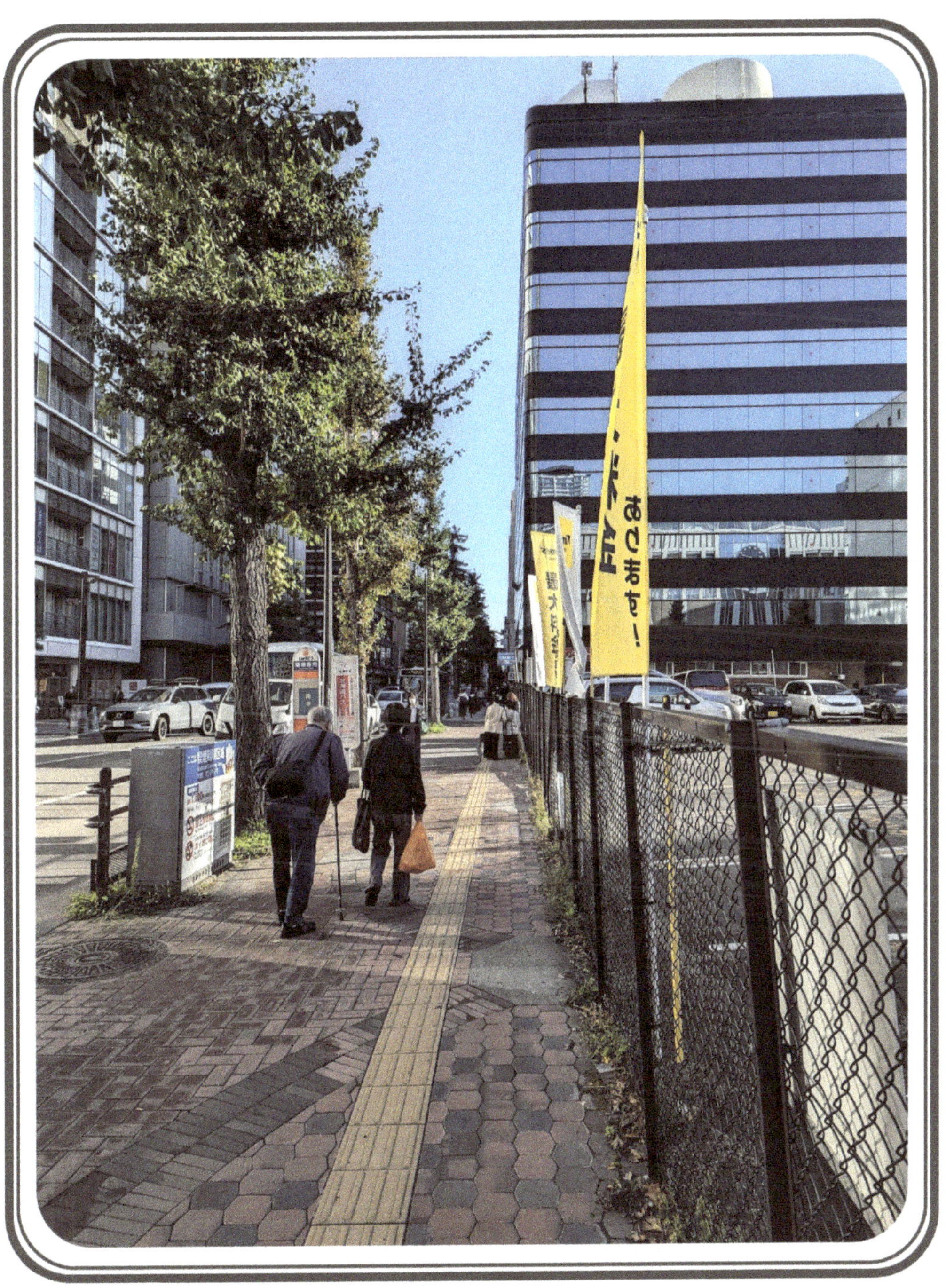

DOROTHY

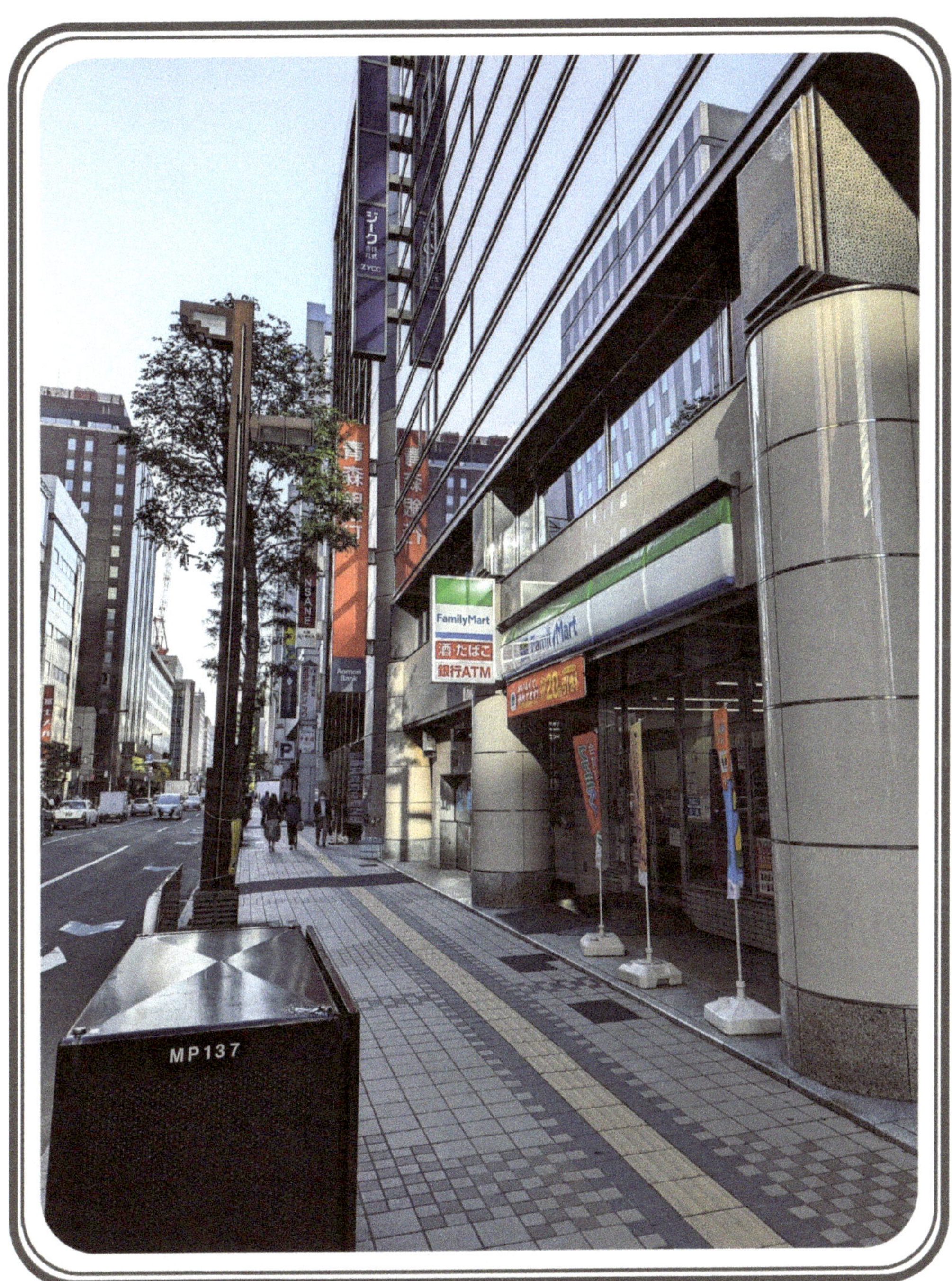
FamilyMart
酒・たばこ
銀行ATM
Aomori Bank
MP137

STELLAR

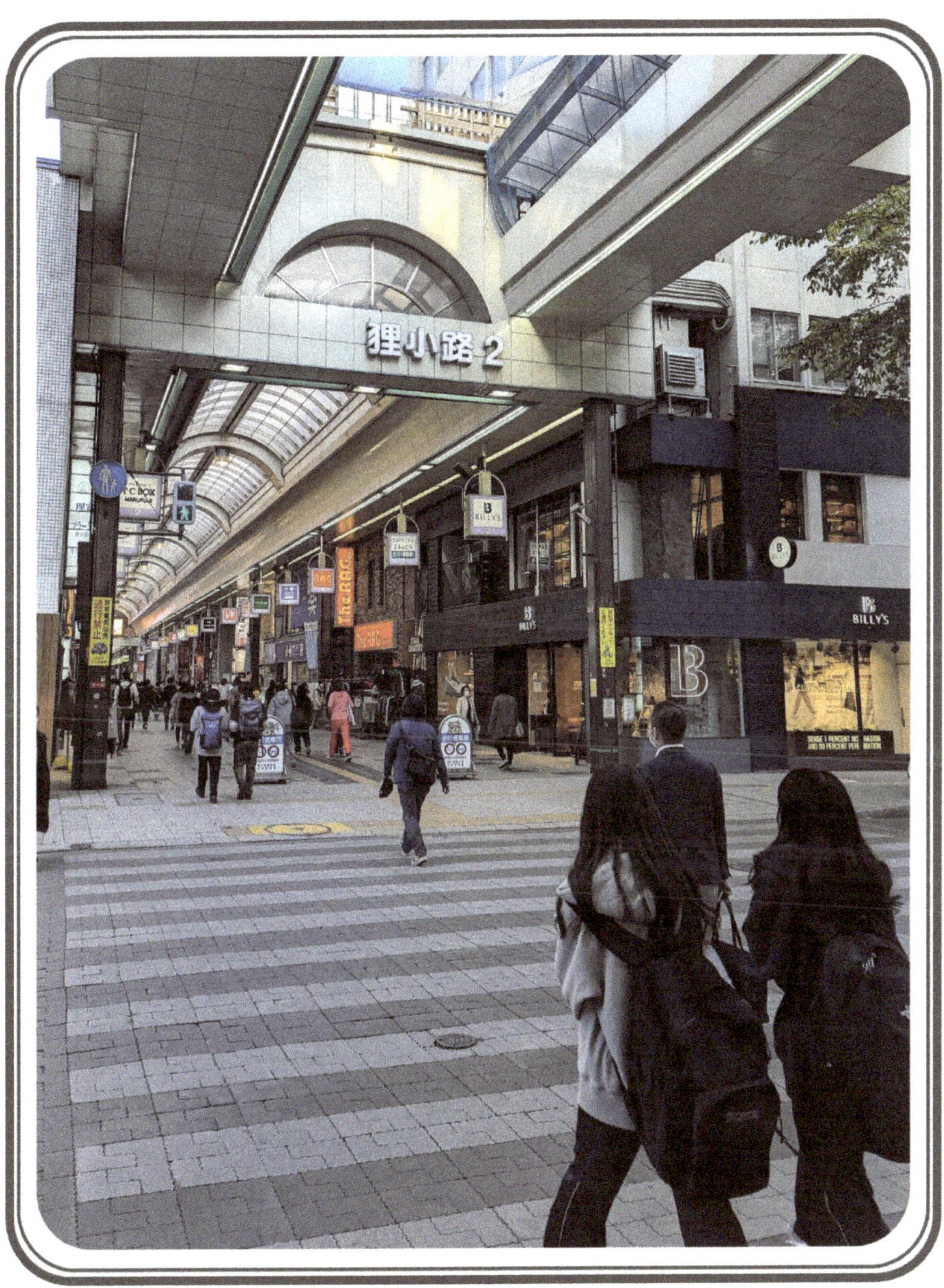
狸小路 2
BILLY'S

BURROW

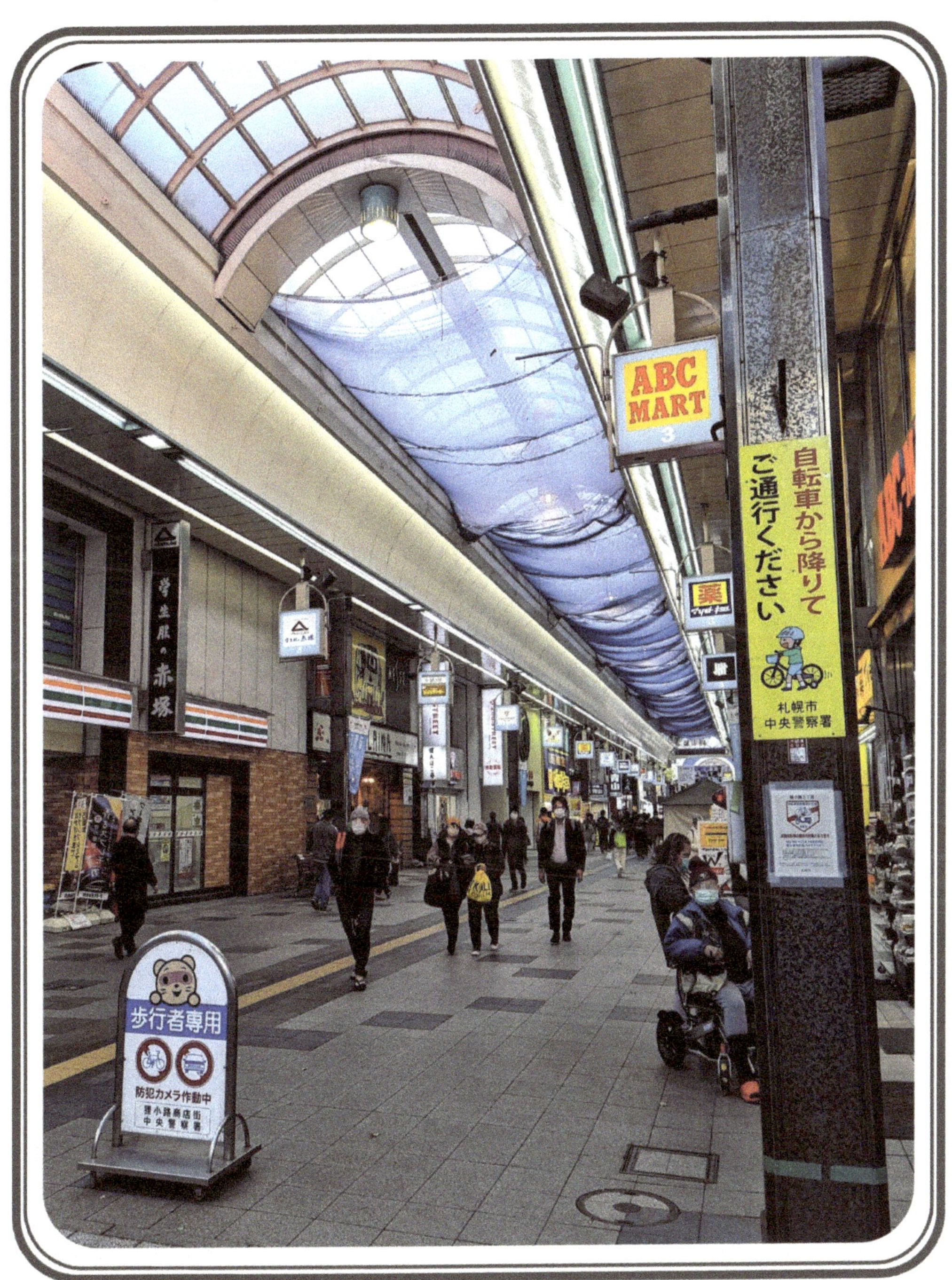
ABC MART
自転車から降りて
ご通行ください
札幌市
中央警察署
学生服の赤塚
薬
歩行者専用
防犯カメラ作動中
狸小路商店街
中央警察署

BENEFACTION

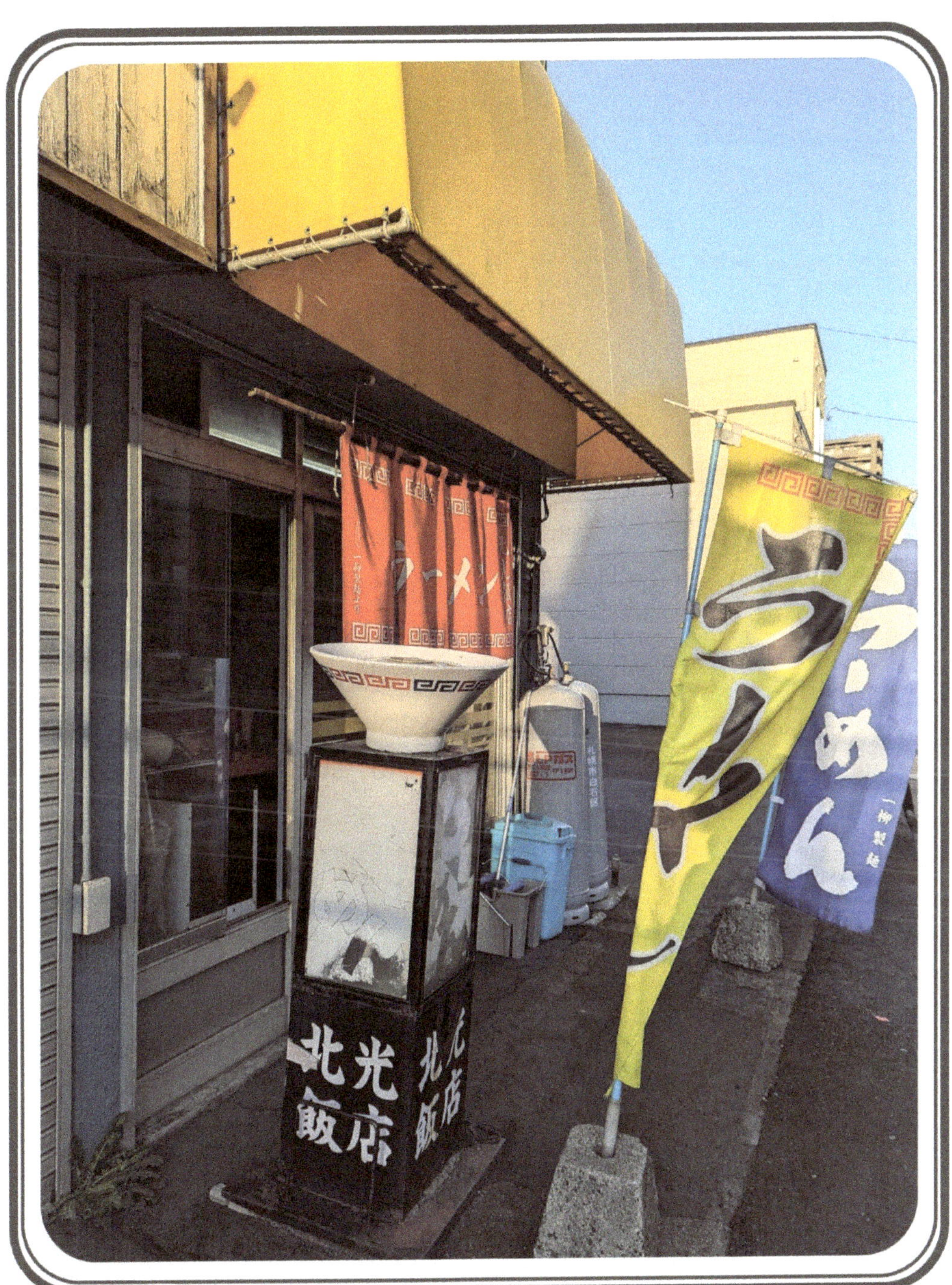

ラーメン
北光飯店

YUM

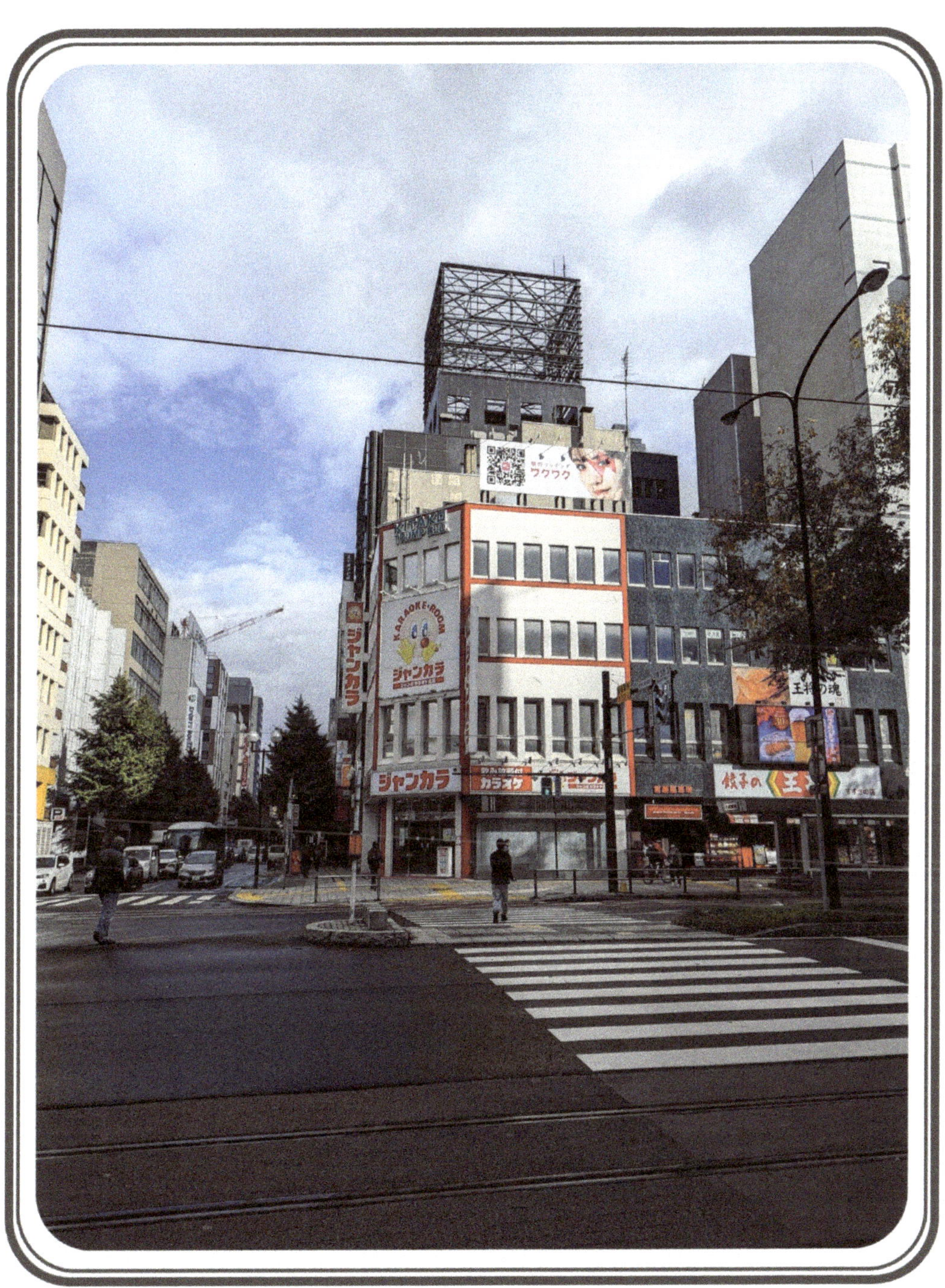

ワクワク
KARAOKE-ROOM
ジャンカラ
ジャンカラ
ジャンカラ
カラオケ
王将の魂

PARENTING

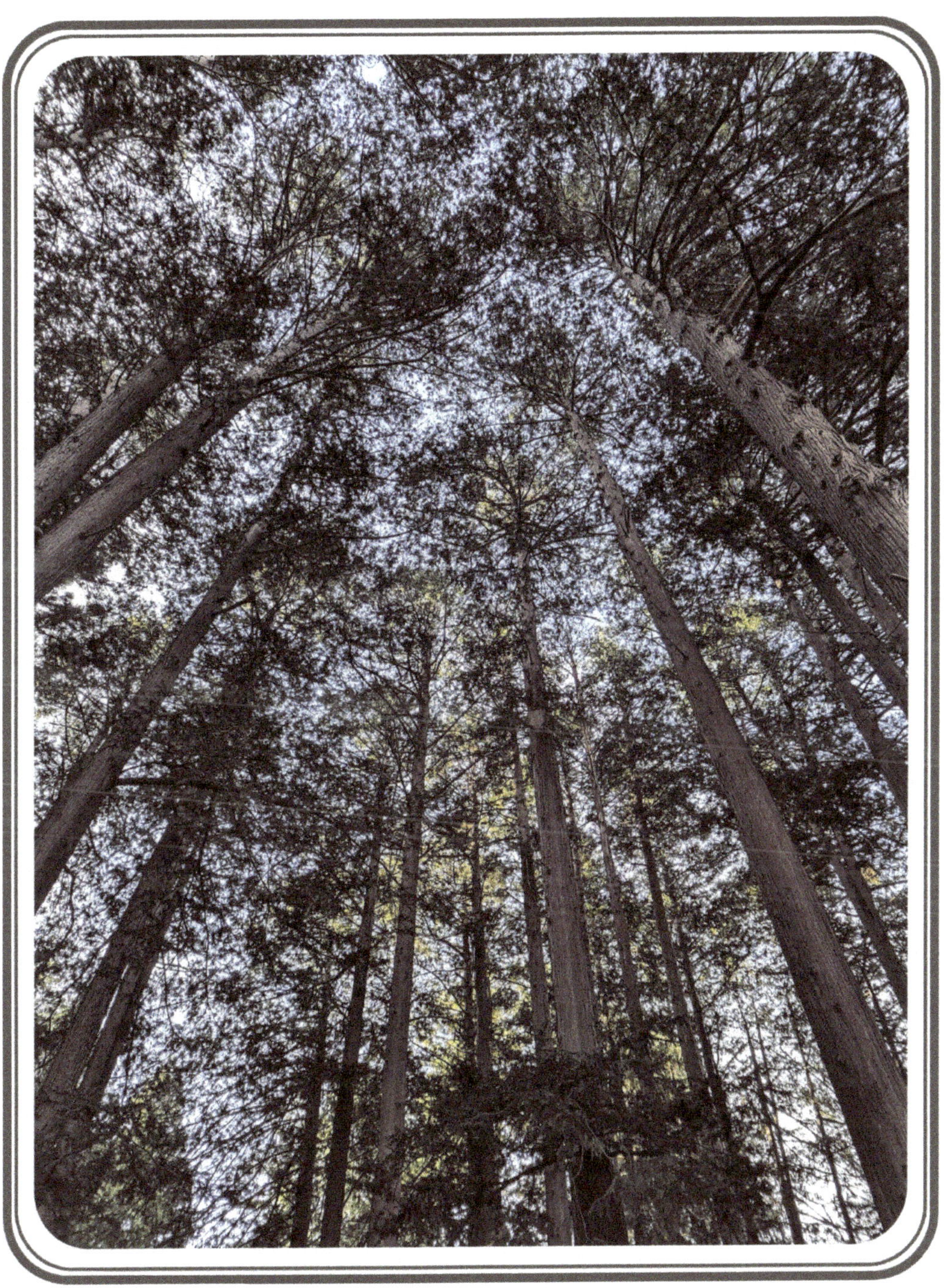

GORSE

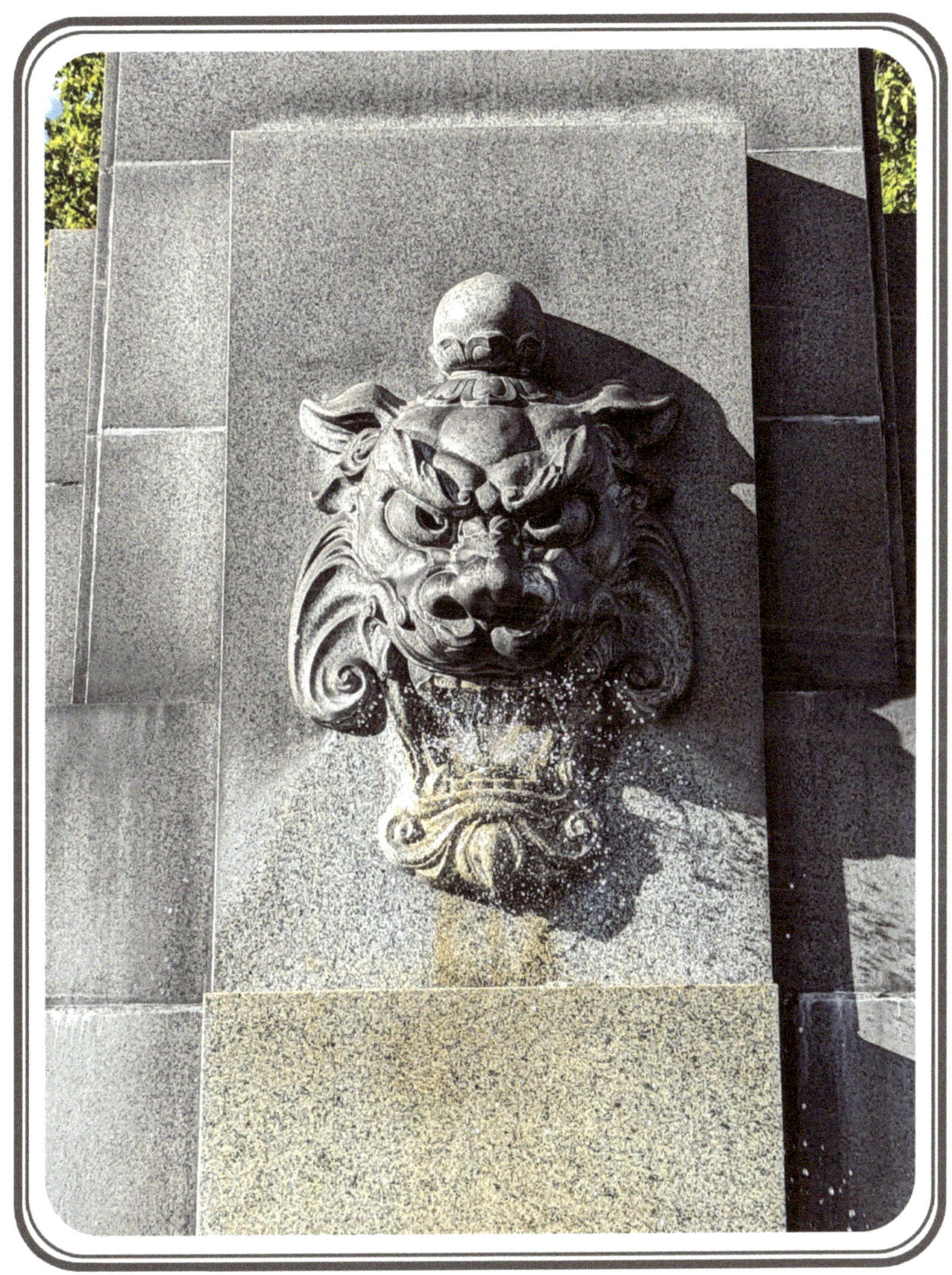

COPSE

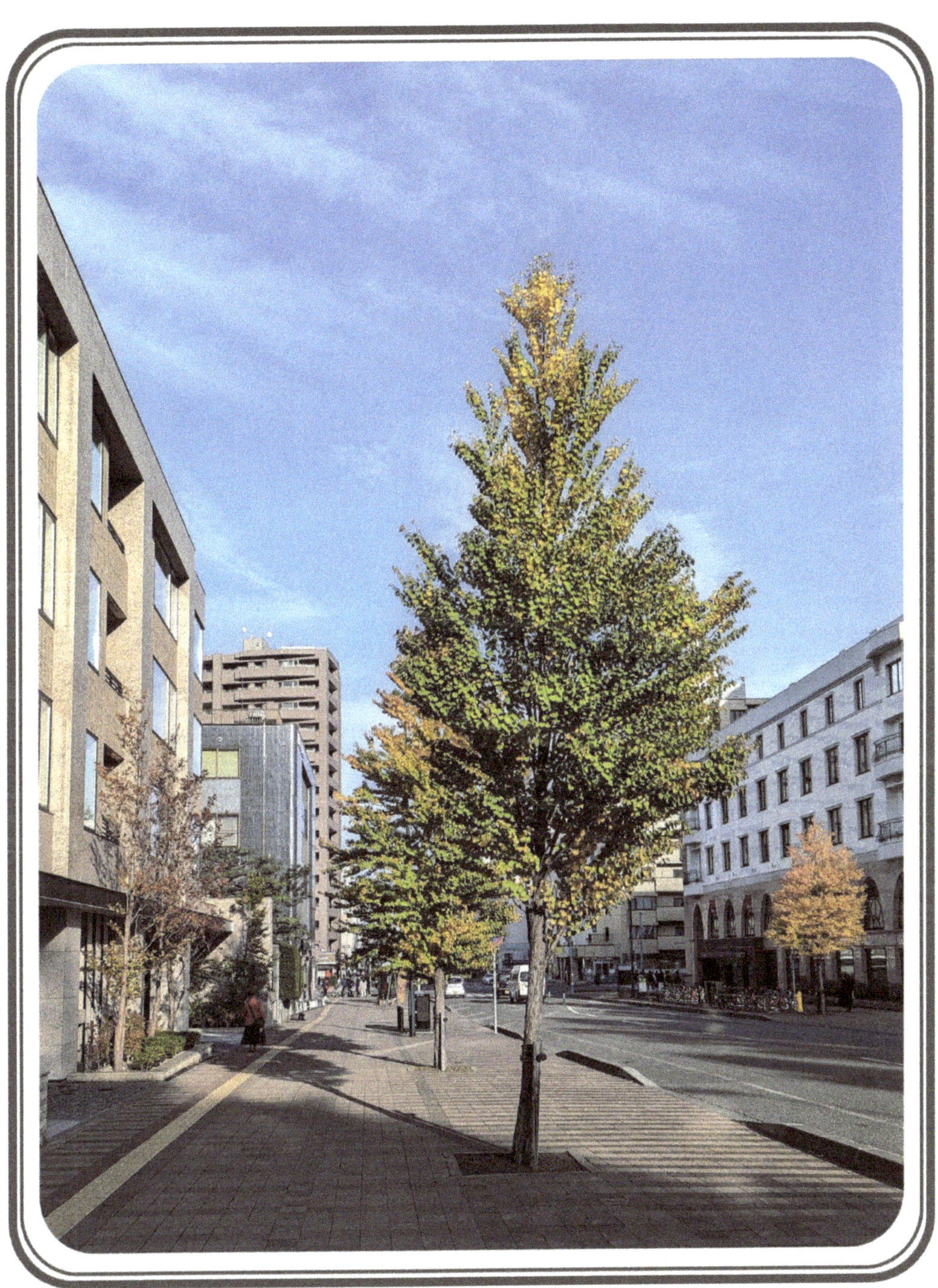

METRICAL

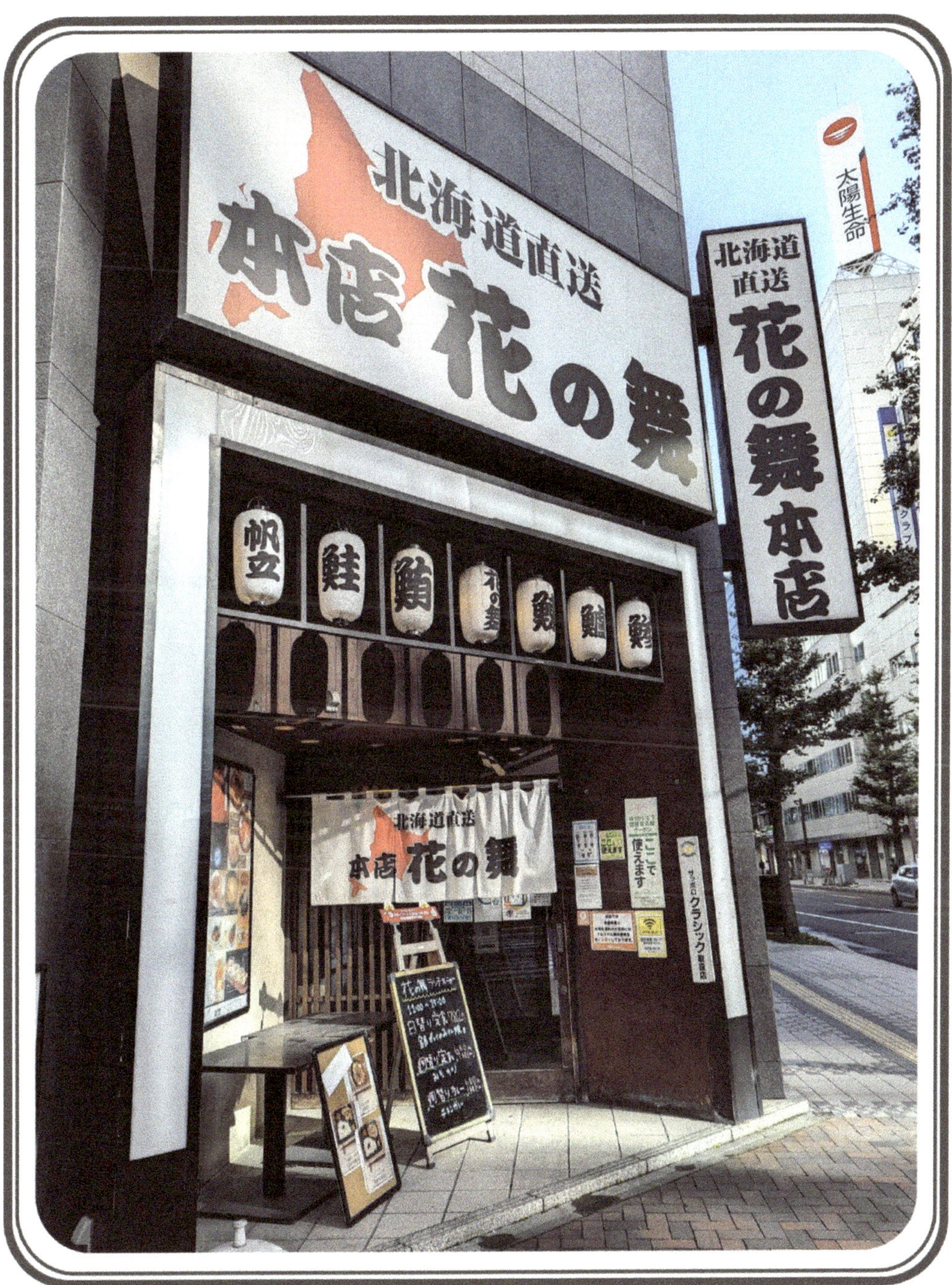
北海道直送
本店
花の舞
北海道直送
花の舞本店
太陽生命
帆立
鮭
北海道直送
本店 花の舞
ここで使えます
サッポロ クラシック

WYETH

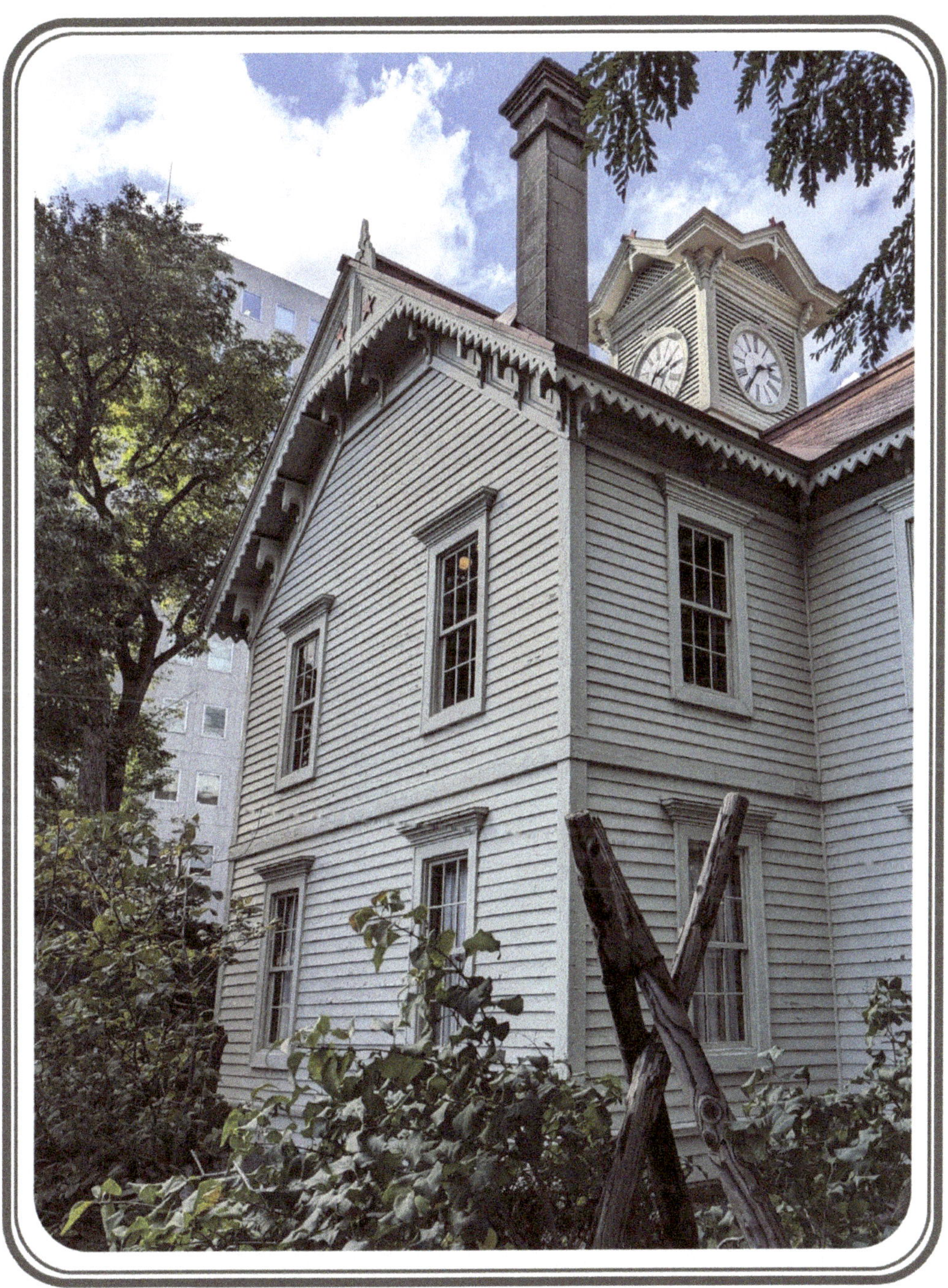

FLOW

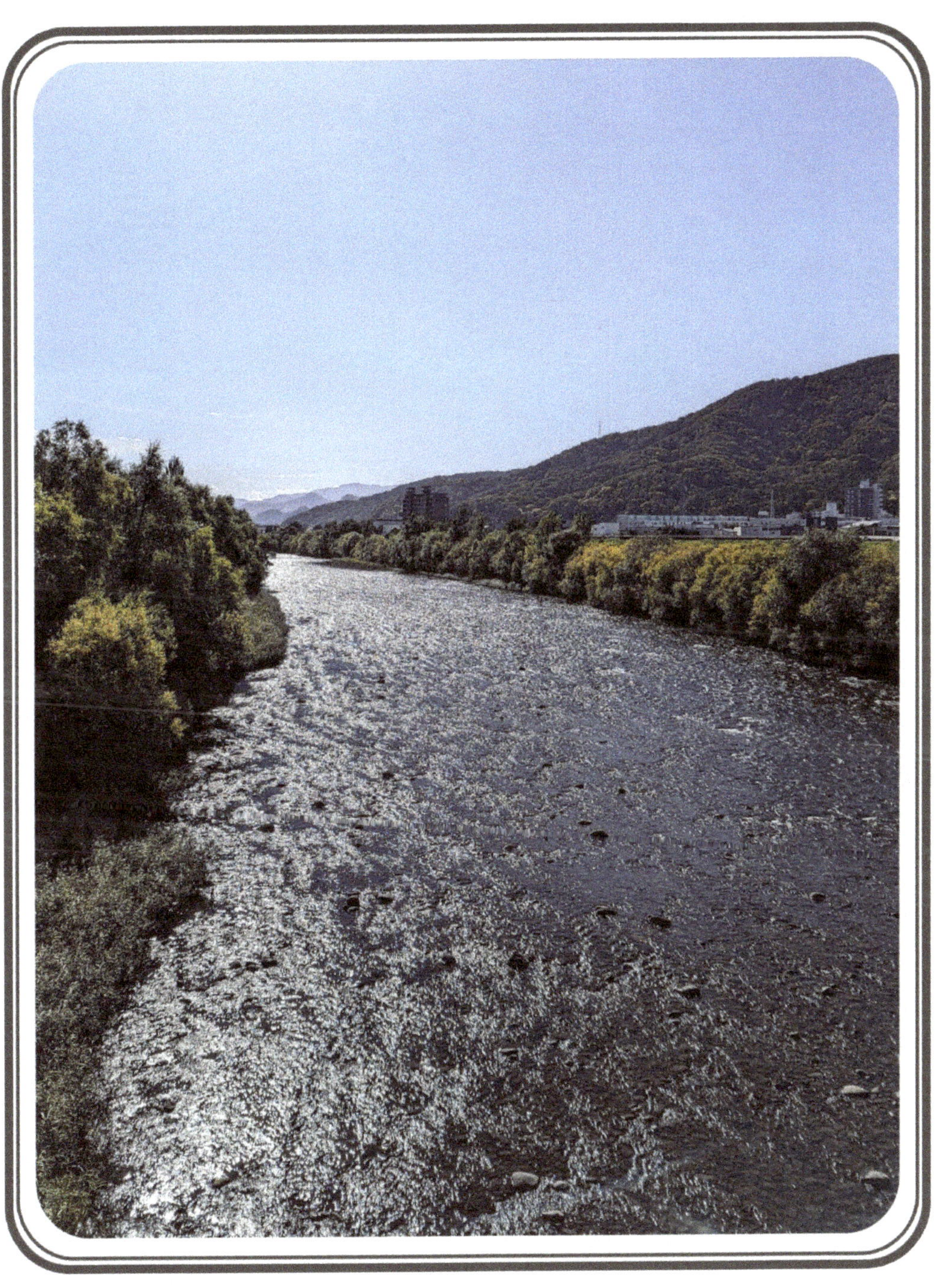

TITLES IN THIS SERIES

Gardens of Sapporo, Japan
Mt. Moiwa, Sapporo, Japan
Shrines of Sapporo, Japan
Parks of Sapporo, Japan
Sapporo City, Japan

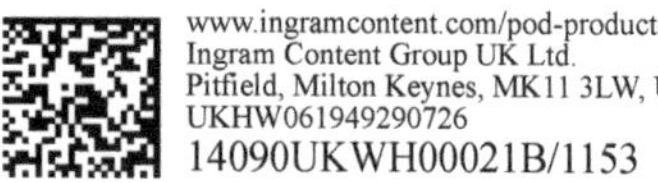
www.ingramcontent.com/pod-product-compliance
Ingram Content Group UK Ltd.
Pitfield, Milton Keynes, MK11 3LW, UK
UKHW061949290726
14090UKWH00021B/1153

9 781951 389291